The Anti-Philosophers

The
Anti-Philosophers

A STUDY OF THE PHILOSOPHES
IN EIGHTEENTH-CENTURY FRANCE

R. J. White

Macmillan
St. Martin's Press

First published 1970 by
MACMILLAN AND CO LTD
Little Essex Street London W C 2
and also at Bombay Calcutta and Madras
Macmillan South Africa (Publishers) Pty Ltd Johannesburg
The Macmillan Company of Australia Pty Ltd Melbourne
The Macmillan Company of Canada Ltd Toronto
St Martin's Press Inc New York
Gill and Macmillan Ltd Dublin
Library of congress Catalog card no. 77-93580

Printed in Great Britain by
R. & R. CLARK LTD
Edinburgh

CONTENTS

Contents

LIST OF PLATES

BETWEEN PAGES 64 AND 65

ACKNOWLEDGEMENTS

The publishers wish to thank the following, who have provided the photographs for the illustrations: 2a, Archives Photographiques; 6, Bibliothèque Nationale; 5, Photographie Bulloz; 1, 3, 4, Photographie Giraudon; 7, Mansell Collection; 2b, 8, Réunion des Musées Nationaux.

PART I

Philosophes
and Philosophers

Chapter One

THE GRAND CHAIN

There is little or nothing in common between the philosophe *and the philosopher.*

MICHAEL OAKESHOTT

In the winter of 1755, M. and Madame Helvétius gave a grand ball at their house in the Rue Sainte-Anne. *Tout le monde de Paris* was there, and the dance was led out by M. Bernard le Bouvier de Fontenelle and Élisabeth Helvétius. M. de Fontenelle was ninety-eight. Élisabeth Helvétius was three. *La vieillesse et la jeunesse, le vieillard et l'enfant,* or – as some said – Beauty and the Beast. At any rate, diverse types of the philosopher. M. de Fontenelle, hobbling along on his spindleshanks, was very much the philosopher as the century, in France, understood the term. His achievement was the product of steady and studied collectivity. Little Élisabeth Helvétius was only a philosopher in the Wordsworthian meaning of the term, a meaning the century never learnt to recognise:

> Thou, whose exterior semblance doth belie
> Thy soul's immensity;
> Thou best Philosopher . . . Mighty Prophet! Seer blest!

At the moment she was hopping along beside an animated mummy, and pinching his almost fleshless shins in order to tell him when the music stopped and when it went on again. *Ce n'est que le premier pas qui coûte,* M. de Fontenelle might have been heard to murmur, adding in a reedy whisper: *et le dernier?* Not that he was the man to give in. The story had long been told in Paris of his apology when, at the age of eighty-nine, he had burst at an inappropriate moment into the boudoir of Madame Helvétius, Élisabeth's beautiful mother. *'Ah! Madame,'* he had said, 'if I were only eighty!' Descended from a sister of the great Pierre Corneille, he had been about the same age as little Élisabeth

Helvétius when Louis XIV began his personal rule over France. He had published his most famous work, a popular account of the stellar universe for women,[1] seventy years ago, when he was just a year short of thirty. Now the doyen of the *Philosophes*, he was still going strong. He was not to give up the ghost until he was within a month of his hundredth birthday, which was rather more than a year too soon for him to see the publication of his host's masterpiece, *De l'esprit*. Thus, as M. de Fontenelle hobbled along beside the little Élisabeth, the generations of *Philosophes* joined hands in the intellectual Grand Chain extending from the Age of Louis XIV to the Age of the French Revolution. Thus, it might also be said, the *Philosophes* advertised the health-giving properties of their philosophy.

The use of the term *Philosophe* has been narrowed down from its dictionary meaning of philosopher in general to serve as the name of a specific breed or genus of philosopher which flourished in France in the eighteenth century. Its leading figures were Diderot and d'Alembert, the *'Encyclopédistes'*,[2] principal luminaries of the 'Enlightenment' which is supposed to have dawned on a benighted world in the age immediately preceding the outbreak of the French Revolution, whose intellectual precursors the *Philosophes* were. Used with a capital 'P' and lumped together as an intellectual School, the *Philosophes* assume a common character as distinctive as that of the 'Physiocrats' or the 'Utilitarians'. They are distinctive if only because of their community in opposition to the *ancien régime*, their wholly irreverent temper, their contempt or neglect of the faith and intellect of their forefathers, of all that was old and long-established, in short their 'infidelity'. Perhaps their character may best be judged from the proportion of space accorded to established modes of thought by d'Alembert in the *Discours préliminaire* which he wrote for the Encyclopedia in 1751. In this brief and brilliant summary of intellectual history nothing much is said of anything before the Renaissance, and the only great thinkers who figure in the survey are Bacon, Descartes, Newton, Locke and Leibniz. In the table, or chart of *'les connaissances humaines'* about one inch out of thirteen is given to theology and religion, while the rest is devoted to 'positive knowledge'.

[1] *Entretiens sur la pluralité des mondes*, first published 1686. The editions that came out during Fontenelle's lifetime, and the variant texts, may be studied in the introduction to Robert Shackleton's edition, published by the Clarendon Press in 1955; see especially pp. 40–8.

[2] Joint editors, and authors of a large part, of *L'Encyclopédie*, 1751–65, in seventeen volumes.

Divine Philosophy, *la science de Dieu*, gets about as much space as iron manufacture.

The positive tenets of the *Philosophes* were less unanimously held but may perhaps be summarised a trifle vaguely as devotion to liberality and toleration. They believed, as Lord Morley said, 'that human nature is good, that the world is capable of being made a desirable abiding-place, and that the evil of the world is the fruit of bad education and bad institutions'. Morley was writing in 1878, and he felt able to add: 'This cheerful doctrine now strikes on the ear as a commonplace and a truism.' In some quarters, notably those presided over by twentieth-century *Philosophes* like Bertrand Russell and the late H. G. Wells, it does so still. The *Philosophe*, like the Gentleman, the Bourgeois, the *Uomo Universale*, is eternal. In the eighteenth century, however, they were never a party, a school, a single movement, however much their enemies deplored them as such, Burke calling them a 'cabal', Coleridge a 'sect'. No one, not even their friends and allies, would deny their sectarian spirit. They were not as a rule admitted to learned bodies where true philosophers habited. Charles Pinot Duclos, when he became Secretary of the Académie Française, was all for intellectuals and *gens d'esprit*, but not for *Philosophes*. He persisted in excluding Diderot.

Perhaps it would be best to say of the *Philosophes* that they were united only in the fact that they shared a certain cast of intellectual countenance or bore a certain common mental aspect. The least convincing bond between them is that of class, the notion that they were 'the intellectual spearhead of the bourgeoisie'. To speak of their affiliation with the bourgeoisie is to say no more than that they were French. They were recruited from all levels of society, except, as might be imagined, the lowest. The greatest of them was the son of a master-cutler, Denis Diderot being embued with a deep respect for, and knowledge of, technology, which is why the great *Encyclopédie* was adorned by eleven volumes of engravings, chiefly of the arts and manufactures of France. Fontenelle and Voltaire were both sons of well-to-do advocates, Buffon, Montesquieu and Condillac were sons of the *noblesse de robe*, and d'Alembert was the love-child of a soldier and a nun of good family. Helvétius was the son of a wealthy physician who once performed the dubiously useful feat of curing Louis XV and became court-physician to Queen Marie Leczinska. He himself was known as 'the spoilt child of finance and fashion', and for years was a wealthy farmer-general. La Mettrie was the son of a wealthy merchant of St-Malo. Paul Thiry, Baron d'Holbach, was an immigrant from the Palatinate. Condorcet was a marquis who

escaped the guillotine in the Revolution, it is thought, only by commit-
ting suicide in prison. And so they go on, a roll-call of characters from
all the principal regions of French society.

It was Diderot who painted the portrait of the *Philosophe* in the article
Philosophe which he wrote for the Encyclopedia. As may be expected it was considerably idealised, for he was after all painting a self-
portrait. He says little about any claims to technical expertise in the
science of philosophy, though some *Philosophes*, notably Montesquieu,
Condillac and Diderot himself in his early works, are by no means
devoid of such claims. What he is principally concerned to emphasise
is their sociability, their devotion to the well-being and happiness of their
fellow-men. It was by such devotion he thought that they would deserve
immortality. They were sustained in sacrificing themselves in the cause
of humanity by the comforting thought of their being remembered by
men of education and good-will in future generations. This was the only
form of personal immortality in which they could believe.[1] The only
divinity on earth for the *Philosophe* was civil society, and Reason was for
him what Grace was for the Christian. The *Philosophe* lived in and for
civil society. Virtue for him was a combination of moral probity and an
exact attention to social duties. He was no mere brain, no naked conscience. He cultivated good morals (*les mœurs*) with a rational mind
properly disposed to reflection and precision. He could say with Renaissance man: *Homo sum, humani a me nihil alienum puto*. In painting this
glowing picture, Diderot was in the first place eulogising the humani-
tarianism which belonged to his own warm and even sentimental nature,
as it may be seen especially in his choice of favourite pictures in his
Salons,[2] and in his readiness to weep and to roar with laughter at slight
provocation. He was also basing himself (sometimes verbally) on an
anonymous article written in 1743.[3] It was not always so. Early in the
eighteenth century the name *Philosophe* was a term of reproach. When
Muralt wrote of the species at the beginning of the century a *Philosophe*
was taken to be a man who wished to live in moody and invidious solitude.
By 1750 all this was changed and the name had a pleasing connotation.
The great thinkers of the previous century – perhaps of all centuries –

[1] This concept of immortality comes in his article Encyclopedie for the Encyclopedia.

[2] Diderot's notices of painting, etc., exhibited in the Salons de l'Académie Royale,
1759–81, have been presented in four volumes by Jean Seznec and J. Adhémar (Oxford,
1957–67).

[3] See '*Le Philosophe*, texts and interpretation', ed. H. Dieckmann, *Washington University Studies*, new series: 'Language and Literature, no. 18' (St Louis, 1948).

had been great solitaries, generally lacking interest in the application of their ideas and little concerned with the well-being of the human race. Now in order to lay claim to the title *Philosophe* there was no need to be a philosophical specialist or a technical expert in ideas, the author of a system or the creator of a comprehensive interpretation of the world. One needed to be a lover of mankind and a fighter for humanity's well-being, a devotee of reason and an enemy of prejudice. It was especially important to be the foe of *l'infâme*.

That is why the *Philosophe* has come to be the opposite of a philosopher, hardly more a philosopher than Duke Ellington is a duke or Count Basie a count. The distinction has been discussed pejoratively for the *Philosophe* by a modern philosopher zealously concerned for the name and fame of his *couvent*,[1] or, in the contemporary idiom, his 'empire'. Some quarter of a century ago, in the introduction to a treatise on *Experience and its Modes*, Michael Oakeshott undertook to rescue philosophy from a perennial threat of degradation at the hands of 'practical' men, taking up a task which had frequently occupied the most famous of his predecessors, S. T. Coleridge. In an age of Utilitarian 'philosophy', the poet had devoted much intellectual energy to the exposure of what he called 'the usurpation of that venerable name by physical and psychological empiricism'. The very terms of ancient wisdom, he complained, were worn out, or, 'far worse, stamped on baser metal'. Even supposedly educated men had come to use such sacred terms as 'idea' in a way that would have caused Platonists of all ages to turn in their graves. Mere clowns like Holofernes and Costard,[2] posing as Metaphysics and Common Sense, were assuring themselves and the world that modern philosophers had 'exploded all ideas but those of sensation'. Nor was this surprising in an age when the chemist, Sir Humphrey Davy, could write his *confessio fidei* under the title *Consolations of Travel, or the Last Days of a Philosopher*, or an advocate of the factory-system (Alexander Ure) compose a treatise under the title *The Philosophy of Manufacture*. 'From a popular philosophy and a philosophic populace Good Sense deliver us', Coleridge prayed. 'The root of the evil is a public', he believed, and before long 'we shall come round to the esoteric (interior, hidden) doctrine of the ancients', and 'learn to under-

---

1 'Voltaire . . . est comme les moines qui n'écrivent pas pour le sujet qu'ils traitent, mais pour la gloire de leurordre. Voltaire écrit pour son couvent.' (Montesquieu, *Pensées diverses*.)

2 The schoolmaster and the clown in Shakespeare's *Love's Labour's Lost*. See Coleridge's first *Lay Sermon*.

stand what Christ meant when He commanded us not to cast pearls before swine'.

Professor Oakeshott, despite the fact that he was writing in the genera, tion of Dr Joad and the first B.B.C. Brains Trust, resisted this mood of dejection. He was content to deplore the irrelevant impulses that often arouse people to take an interest in philosophy: the desire for a gospel, for guidance in arriving at values, for some clue to the mystery of existence, or merely for assurance that there is nothing degrading in one's being alive. For all such people, he would say, 'thinking is at first associated with an extraneous desire for *action*', the itch to do something about things, and to know what to do. Knowing what to do, of course, depends upon knowing the facts, and the *Philosophes* were voracious collectors and purveyors of information. Their great Encyclopedia, in seventeen volumes, each containing some 900 double-column pages, along with eleven volumes of plates, might be regarded, from one angle, as a vast book of instructions, an extended manual of the kind supplied with a do-it-yourself kit, for although the work includes a great deal of profes, sional instruction in philosophy and the natural sciences, it excels as a descriptive handbook of technology. Voltaire's story in *Le Taureau blanc* of the royal dinner party where Louis XV sent two footmen to fetch the weighty volumes in order to settle the question of how gun, powder was manufactured, and Madame de Pompadour's queries about the manufacture of rouge and silk stockings, ending up with the lordly confession that the suspect work was a great national asset (even if their lordships did not detect its quality as itself comprising gunpowder), may not be strictly true, but it deserves to be, for it sums up a great epoch of modern history with the touch of genius. It was possible to learn from the Encyclopedia how to do anything from the casting of cannon to the making of pastry, from governing a kingdom to falconry. The technical diagrams were made under Diderot's supervision, and people soon dis, covered that this monument of philosophy was also an indispensable 'Inquire Within' for everyone engaged in the world's business, from the merchant to the craftsman. Obviously such a work had to be written straightforwardly, eschewing technical or 'learned' language as far as possible, the kind of writing the self-styled 'learned world' suspects. More especially is this style and its purposes suspect to the professional philosopher who, as Diderot did not hesitate to declare, favours a certain obscurity of style. As for simplification for the understandings of common men, it is to be distrusted as the parent of misrepresentation. It may very well be true, as Oscar Wilde said, that truth is never pure and seldom simple, but the *Philosophes* were resolved to make it both. They were determined to be read, and read easily, like good journalists, certainly like good Frenchmen in the tradition of their great master, René Descartes, who despite his profundity had been known truly in his day, like William Shakespeare, as 'that pleasant wit'. Descartes's first principle was the acceptance only of clear and distinct ideas. He was avowedly addressing himself not to his fellow-philosophers, but to his fellow-citizens. For that reason, again, he wrote his *Discours* in French, in as good, clear, straightforward French as he could muster. The vehicle for his thought was ready to his hand. In his use of it he set an example which his disciples (and the *Philosophes* were his disciples) copied to the everlasting and common fame of their works. One of the unacknowledged reasons why dons at the older universities have tended to distrust French translation as an adequate test of linguistic ability for entrance examinations is the fact, as one such don was heard to complain, that ' You can't set a passage of *difficult* French . . . it doesn't exist.'

Nothing in the character of the *Philosophes* exasperates the philosopher more than this, their intense practicality, their clarity, their passion for exact information about everything under the sun. One of the prime obnoxious characteristics of the breed, according to Oakeshott, is their 'peculiar confidence in knowledge', what he calls their 'hydroptic thirst' for information about the present world and its creatures. Such a thirst, he goes on to declare, is only possible in a world where there is a 'certain rude copiousness about the supply'. Its indiscriminate nature, its superficiality, its almost savage character, reminds him of a September orchard when a swarm of wasps have passed that way. Like the wasps, the *Philosophes* pillage the world of knowledge in 'senseless depredation', utterly unconscious of their vulgarity and of the possibility of their own disenchantment. Only gradually do men learn that philosophy is without any direct bearing on the practical conduct of life. The original error of thinking otherwise owes a great deal to the unfortunate example of certain so-called 'philosophers' actually *Philosophes*, who have harboured some purpose foreign to philosophy, the purpose of the preacher, for instance, or the reformer. Philosophy, Oakeshott would contend,

> depends for its existence upon maintaining its independence of all extraneous interests, and in particular from the practical interest. To popularize philosophy is at once to debase it: a general demand for philosophy is a general demand for degradation. . . .

We must conclude, then, that all attempts whatever to find some practi¬
cal justification for philosophical thought and the pursuit of philoso¬
phical truth, all attempts to replace life with philosophy by subjecting
life to the criticism of philosophy, must be set aside as misguided

> . . . instead of a gospel, the most philosophy can offer us (in respect of
> practical life) is an escape, perhaps the only complete escape open to
> us.

By this reckoning, it is evident that the *Philosophes*, those leading figures
of French intellectual history in the eighteenth century, embody all the
defects or shortcomings which disqualify men from claiming the title of
Philosopher. Professor Oakeshott delivered his judgement in the words:
'there is little or nothing in common between the philosopher and the
philosophe'. For the *Philosophes* were, after all, concerned above all else
to preach a gospel, to establish a rationale of reform, to change the world,
to do precisely what Karl Marx (their most notable successor) in a famous
aphorism said it was time that philosophers should do. 'Hitherto philoso¬
phers have only interpreted the world in various ways,' he said, 'but the
real task is to alter it.' On Oakeshott's premises this is a task not for
philosophers but for *Philosophes*. The primary conviction of the *Philoso¬
phes* was that their kind of activity was above all else practical. They were,
of all men, *hommes engagés*, men with a mission, deeply concerned with
social purpose. The philosopher might dwell on the mountain¬tops.
Indeed, the great philosophers have for the most part been great solitar¬
ies, and perhaps that is a cause and an effect of their so often having been
bachelors.[1] As Diderot expressed it in his *Pensées sur l'interprétation de la
nature* (1753):

> The speculative *Philosophe* is like one who looks out from mountain¬
> tops hidden in the clouds: the features of the lowlands have dis¬
> appeared, and he sees only his own thoughts, the eminence to which
> he has risen – and to which few are able to follow him, and where few
> can breathe.

For, as the great *Philosophe* recognised, 'Great abstractions admit of but
a sombre light.' The very act of generalisation, by its nature, tends to
deprive concepts of sensible form. Pure ideas, defecated of material form,
are not everybody's meat. For the people at large they are only to be
apprehended in terms of their utility.

There is only one way of commending philosophy to the common man,
and that is by showing him its usefulness. He always asks of a thing:

[1] Hobbes, Locke, Descartes, Hume, Kant, Hegel . . .

what use is it? And one should never be in the position of having to
reply – none. He doesn't realise that what enlightens the philosopher
and what is useful to the common man are very different things, since
the understanding of the philosopher is often enlightened by what
obscures the mind of the common man and his mind is darkened by
what the common man finds useful.

He suspected that there is a sort of obscurity that one might call 'the
affectation of the Great Masters', a kind of veil which it pleases them to
draw between mankind and the face of nature. He even professed to
believe that another month's work by Newton on his *Principia* would have
rendered it clear to the common intelligence. This accessibility to the
minds of ordinary people was vitally important to the *Philosophes*. 'Let
us hasten to popularise philosophy', the great editor of the Encyclopedia
is always crying. And if anyone protests that his work is unsuited to be
put before common men – *'qu'on ne mettra jamais à la portée du commun
des esprits'* – then it will become obvious that the author lacks *'la bonne
methode'* and sufficient practice (*'la longue habitude'*). As for the danger
of popularisation resulting in 'plebification' or degradation, the *Philosophe* was more than prepared to take the chance. His concern was, after
all, with *haute vulgarisation*. He was, nine times out of ten, a literary man,
even a journalist. Ivory towers on mountain-tops were not for him. When
Diderot and d'Alembert presented their Encyclopedia, the title-page
ascribed its management, editorship and authorship not to philosophers
or savants, but to 'a society of men of letters'.

The historic function of the *Philosophes* was not to originate new ideas
but to translate the ideas of the previous century ('The Century of
Genius')[1] into the language of every day for everyday men, and women.
As Professor Butterfield has written,

> the great movement of the eighteenth century was a literary one – it
> was not the new discoveries of science in that epoch but, rather, the
> French *philosophe* movement that determined the course Western
> civilisation was to take. The discoveries of seventeenth century science
> were translated into a new outlook and a new world-view, not by
> scientists themselves, but by the heirs and successors of Fontenelle.

[1] Alfred North Whitehead went so far as to say that Europe over the past two and a
half centuries has been living on the accumulated intellectual capital of 'The Century
of Genius' (*Science and the Modern World*, 1925, ch. III).

Chapter Two

FONTENELLE

'*Quoi!*' *s'écriaitelle, 'j'ai dans la tête tout la système de l'univers!*
Je suis savante!' '*Oui!*' *repliquaije, 'vous l'êtes assez raisonnable*
ment . . .'

Master and pupil at the end of the sixth
evening in *La Pluralité des mondes*

BERNARD LE BOVIER DE FONTENELLE was the first of the *Philosophes*
and very nearly the last of them. His lifespan (1657–1757) enclosed all
the notable ones. He was their prototype, their founder and finally their
doyen. He represents their wit, their levity, their journalistic expertise,
their sociability, their refusal to change. He had also some qualities they
generally lacked: a certain cynicism, a total scepticism, a notable dis-
regard for the human condition. He was never *engagé*, save in the matter
of the comfort of M. de Fontenelle. They were like dogs, quarrelsome,
rather noisy, incorrigibly frisky. He was more like a cat, neat, selfish,
cold, insinuating. It was said that when he had been in a room he left
behind no traces of his having been there. He clung indomitably to his
own tastes. For instance, he liked his asparagus served in olive oil. When
he entertained the Abbé Terranon, who preferred it served in butter,
and the Abbé fell down in a fit, Fontenelle at once ran to the kitchen to
instruct the cook to serve the dish in oil: '*Tout à l'huile!*' he cried.
'All in oil!' He had a remarkable head, but it was said that he had no
heart. 'It's a brain that you've got in there,' Madame de Tencin once
said, tapping him on the breast. Nor was he ever seen to weep, or to run,
and when asked why he never laughed, he replied: '*Non, je ne fais*
jamais ah, ah, ah.' When he grew old and very deaf and unable to take part
in the conversation he would have remarks repeated to him and then
make his contribution in the third person. 'Fontenelle, he says . . .' He
retained his love of praise to the end as an immensely successful writer.
'I would praise you,' an admirer once said, 'if only I possessed your
subtlety of mind.' 'Never mind,' he replied. 'Praise me all the same . . .'
He was a cold fish, and of course a bachelor.

Beginning early in the reign of Louis XIV, a child of the house of Corneille, he was expected to shine, and set about scintillating with determination from the time that he left his native Rouen, where he had been the model pupil of the Jesuit College. Like Jeremy Bentham, he trained as an advocate and gave up practice after his first brief. Settling in Paris, he devoted himself to journalism and *belles/lettres*, dashing off a great deal of showy verse, some comedies, a tragedy, all in the *libertin* tradition. He attained some success with his *Dialogues of the Dead*, and his *Digression sur les anciens et les modernes*, which was an elegant and forceful contribution to a fashionable controversy, written on the side of the Moderns and still worth reading. He was intent on literary success by *choc*, for, as Voltaire said, 'He always wanted to be witty . . . he couldn't help scintillating.' Yet success hung fire until at the age of twenty/nine he produced his *Entretiens sur la pluralité des mondes*. This was in 1686. It was published in edition after edition, at home and abroad, at least twenty/eight in the author's lifetime. It is generally remembered as *A Dialogue on the Plurality of Inhabited Worlds*, and it made his fortune. Among other things, it is a landmark in the history of space/fiction.

The *libertin* tradition in French literature represented a movement of rebellion against both church and state which showed itself increasingly in the predominantly conformist society of the seventeenth century. *Libertinage* was not concerned with liberation from moral standards. Its representatives like Charles de Saint/Évremond (1616–1703) were con/cerned to reconcile a decorous Epicureanism with an enlightened attachment to Christian doctrine. Some, like La Mothe le Vayer (1588–1672), were free/thinking scholars who developed the humanism of the Renaissance in the direction of scepticism and even paganism. Turbulent spirits like Cyrano de Bergerac (1619–55) composed pleasingly lunatic accounts of space/travel to the sun and the moon. The greatest figure of the *libertin* tradition, however, was undoubtedly its literary ancestor, Michel de Montaigne (1533–92), who had contrived to combine a happy scepticism of outlook (*Que sçais/je?*) with that of a devout Catholic. The gentle genius of Montaigne, the bold fantasy of Cyrano, the gentlemanly Epicureanism of Saint/Évremond (who finally achieved interment in Westminster Abbey), all contributed strands to the *libertin* tradition which ultimately produced Fontenelle.

Ostensibly the *Entretiens* consists of six lectures on the stellar universe for ladies, a genre much in vogue at that time. Fontenelle affects to be the preceptor of a marquise to whom he imparts the delicious mysteries of astronomy in six evenings of walking and talking under the night sky in the grounds of her château near Rouen. The little work thereby acquires an air of gallantry, relating itself (purely theoretically) to the tradition of Héloïse and Abelard, Paolo and Francesca, or (a century later) Julie and Saint-Preux. Not that Fontenelle ever evinces anything more *galant* than a mild and pedantic form of verbal flattery. But the very situation, the star-lit park, the beautiful young woman, the obliging tutor, the general air of intellectual badinage – all alike form a delightful conjunction gratefully romantic in a classical age.

What was the purport of this charming work? Fontenelle was concerned with a form of propaganda, which is what makes him so immediately recognisable as an early *Philosophe*. He wishes to convey the comparative insignificance of the terrestrial globe in the immensity of the universe, that globe on which popes and princes, with their dogmatisms of church and state, parade themselves unaware of the absurdity of their posturings. Fontenelle never says anything explicit of this kind. He leaves it to us to gather it, along with his aristocratic pupil. At the beginning of the sixth and last evening (for like God Fontenelle rested on the seventh) we are admitted to the delicious *chez-soi* feeling of the instructed marquise. Two men of the world who have lately been with her, she tells her preceptor, have been mocking her belief in the truths he has imparted to her, including especially the likelihood that there are other inhabited planets besides our own. Never mind, Fontenelle adjures her: you and I know these things, and the fact that these men of the world do not know them cannot cause any dismay either to us – or to the inhabitants of the other worlds. Personally he is not in the least distressed that Copernicus has displaced man from the central place in the universe. Indeed, he takes pleasure in seeing the earth 'one of the crowd'. He regards quite calmly the desire of most men of the world to put themselves at the centre of the universe, rather in the same way that they are concerned to have the first place at a reception or a ceremony. To them, the presence of a couple of planets will never be so impressive as the presence of a couple of ambassadors. Let them have their little vanities. Let us be content to be an instructed minority. Let us be content to remain a small and select company . . . and not to divulge our mysteries to the people.' Next time they mock her the marquise will reply: 'Ah, if only you knew about the fixed stars!' And anyway not all 'the other worlds', which make our world look small, can diminish the fair eyes and lips of the marquise. *They* will always be well worth while, however many other possible worlds there may be. The recourse to badinage is typical.

Fontenelle's interest in the intellectual welfare of the marquise is minimal. He is principally concerned that the world at large should overhear his lessons. The young lady has an obvious literary value to the writer in the *libertin* tradition. It is a matter of tactics, too, for he knows that the best way to capture the men is through the women. 'We couldn't make a more valuable conquest . . .' he says of the marquise in his dedicatory letter. If wisdom is to present itself to men, under what better guise could it present itself than the guise of the marquise with her youth and beauty? She was, in very deed, an intellectual asset of the first rank. There was nothing in the least original in this, Fontenelle's educational tactic. Not the least intriguing feature of the *Philosophes* is the readiness with which they adopted the propaganda techniques of their enemy, the Roman Church. The control exerted by the priesthood over the masculine sex was well enough understood to follow upon their strategic conquest of wives and mistresses. Moreover, the cult of 'Astronomy for ladies', or more widely 'Science for Women', had been growing throughout the seventeenth century. Molière was to put *Les Femmes savantes* on the stage in 1672, in one of the funniest of his plays. In 1680 the Abbé de Gérard published his *La Philosophie des gens de cour*[1], which went into three editions in five years and contained a wifely obsession with 'celestial studies', the lady's husband lamenting her habit of spending nights on the roof – a fanaticism only to be cured 'by shutting her up in a convent'.[2] Indeed there is reason to believe that Gérard's work was the source of Fontenelle's *Entretiens*. There were even more numerous and more impressive examples of the genre in the subsequent half-century. Among the scientific writings of John Harris, D.D., Fellow and Secretary (briefly) of the Royal Society, and author of the *Lexicon Technicum*, was *Astronomical Dialogues between a Gentleman and a Lady* (1719). Here it is made obvious that Harris's *Lexicon* had served the female sex especially, for the lady puffs that work repeatedly as 'a ready help to me in time of need'. Indeed, she expresses the opinion that 'the Doctor composed it out of a peculiar Regard to our Sex'. Perhaps most famous of all was Francesco Algarotti's *Newtonianismo per le dame*, one edition of which (1739) was dedicated to Fontenelle with the hope that it might equal the success of his *Entretiens*. By the reign of Louis XIV science, including sidereal physics, had become a fad, a hobby, a

[1] Philosophy for courtiers.

[2] Dr Robert Shackleton thinks that Fontenelle was inspired in the *Entretiens* by the desire to refute Gérard's work and 'to rescue the fair sex from its errors'. See the introduction to his edition of the *Entretiens* (Clarendon Press, 1955).

fashionable diversion among men and women of quality. The domestic showcase of physical specimens was no less *comme il faut* than the coffee-table with its latest novels was to be in a later age.

Thierry Maulnier, in an introductory essay to *Les Entretiens*, has remarked on what may be called the author's innocent audacity. At the moment of the most gigantic revolution since Prometheus, a revolution that was to change the rhythm of history and the face of the earth; an adventure far more exalted than the Quest for the Golden Fleece, or the Elixir of Life, or the Philosophers' Stone; a conquest that was to put man in possession of secrets which would make him the master of nature, the ruler of brute forces, the pioneer of a future fraught with limitless possibilities of power; at this moment a young Frenchman of more wit than knowledge entered upon the scene bearing a slender volume on astronomy which could add nothing to human knowledge, but which confined itself to imparting a bright and easy form of knowledge to a young woman. He was engaged in laying down a velvet carpet to the stars for a lady of moderate education and mild curiosity, a young person whose bright eyes would search the heavens and appraise the beauty of the night without terror or surprise, without suspicion that they might conceal the face of God. Instead her response was a pleased cry of 'Ah, *le beau monde!*' like Sophie in Molière's comedy. How indeed was the marquise to know that the horizons of her century concealed the decisive turning-point in the adventure of mankind, the revolution achieved by Descartes, Leibniz and Newton – an infinitely greater affair than the local and temporal revolution which was to take off her granddaughter's head a century later? How was she to know that the fire with which her graceful fingers played was indeed the very fire of Prometheus? Had Fontenelle himself any inkling of this? Was he wholly innocent in his audacity? Certainly, with his pleasingly negligent manner he had already the veiled insolence of the *Philosophe*. At this moment, of all other moments of time, he chose (in Maulnier's words) to descend the steps of a château into the murmurous foliage and waters of a park, a pretty marquise on his arm. There is no hesitation in his step, he is never at a loss for a word. Is his pupil for an instant alarmed at the daring of the thoughts which he proposed? Not so Fontenelle. 'I swear', he assures her, 'that my enthusiasm for these truths is not so great that I would sacrifice to them the very least of the comforts of society.' Zeal, enthusiasm, the sacrifice of social convention to the cause of truth, such things are not in his nature.

The *Entretiens* was published quite openly in France, '*avec privilège du roy'* (or, so to say, under the royal *imprimatur*). If anyone were to accuse him of putting men on the moon, men who could not be descendants of Adam, and thereby exempt from the taint of Original Sin or the necessity of Redemption, he would answer – as he answered beforehand in his Preface: 'I didn't put men there. I only put "inhabitants", who aren't *men* in the least.' If they are not men, it may be asked, what are they? And Fontenelle will reply: 'I have not seen them.' His equivocation is superb, a model for all *Philosophes* to follow. Had he not assured the marquise that he was not disposed to sacrifice the slightest convention of society to the truths of philosophy? None the less, he had lodged the idea in the minds of his readers that there might well exist beings in the universe who had no part in the Christian, let alone the Roman Catholic, scheme of things, and yet who – for all we knew – got on pretty well. The Pope had once partitioned the New World between Spain and Portugal. Would he yet make Catholic claims to the planets? There are rumours that he has done so since the initiation of the Space Age. Perhaps Mrs Meynell was better advised when she composed her *Christ in the Universe*. It is one of the perhaps unintended effects of space-fiction to reduce Christianity to what Hardy's Presences of the Overworld call it, 'a local cult'. Although Fontenelle was not quite writing space-fiction, he was *dans cette galère*, and one of the prime purposes of the *Philosophes* was to make all religions look equally small. Burke, indeed, said the movement was nothing less than 'a conspiracy against Christianity'. Fontenelle took a dignified part in it with his *De l'origine des fables*, which he wrote before 1680 but withheld from publication until 1724, when the Philosophic movement was well afoot. He was in many respects ahead of his age, but it may be said to have caught up with him. His equivocation in *De l'origine des fables* shows all his old cunning: his ostensible subject is the fabulous nature of early man's religious beliefs, but his learned essay in comparative religion is directed against all revealed religions. To conclude his claims as a forerunner of the coming age, it would be well to remember that the next great blow to be struck for relativity in morals by making play with other worlds and the relativity of moral concepts was Voltaire's *Micromégas* in 1752.

The *Entretiens sur la pluralité des mondes* has all the charm, the aesthetic appeal, which make for a successful work of popularisation. This springs not only from the author's literary art and his skilful exploitation of the *libertin* tradition, but also from the inherent attraction of the Cartesian physics from which it is derived. It is impossible to understand the nature of the book's appeal in its age, and for long afterwards, unless one has first grasped the extent to which it was derived from sources infinitely superior to itself. When the marquise echoes the delight of Molière's Sophie, 'Ah, *le beau monde!*[1] I adore its vortices!' she is paying a tribute to the beauty of a scheme of physical science – generally known as Vorticism – which was all the rage among educated people in the seven‹ teenth century. René Descartes, the author of the scheme, was a true philosopher, infinitely superior to the greatest of the *Philosophes*, yet he was their precursor, the genius from whom, as *gens de lettres*, they derived a great part of their force. He lived from 1596 to 1650 and was acclaimed in an *éloge* at the Académie Française within five years of his death as the most revolutionary thinker since Aristotle, the greatest destructive and reconstructive genius for two thousand years. Those who hailed him thus were Frenchmen, and after all Descartes was the maker of the modern French mind. Whatever might happen to the Maginot Line, a patriot said in 1940, France would remain true to herself so long as she preserved the Cartesian line. Descartes seems to us the most French of all Frenchmen largely because he made the French mind what it is, and that in a way no English philosopher – with the possible exception of John Locke – ever made the English, for the English mind was made not by philosophers but by poets.

Descartes's principal claim to fame is his *Essay on Method* of 1636–7, a discourse of some forty pages, which is one of the seminal works of modern history. In it he established the primary duty of philosophic doubt and the exclusive sovereignty of clear and distinct ideas. From Descartes's description of his own rules for the art of thought (and the description of his own rules for the conduct of his own reason is all that he professes to be offering), there may spring a total scepticism and an uninhibited rationalism – though he intended neither. By writing his *Discours* in French he struck the first mighty blow in the battle of the *Philosophes*, addressing himself in easy language to common men. His first words are 'Good sense', and good sense he asserts to be 'of all things in the world the most equally distributed'. A few sentences later he is equating good sense with reason. At a blow he has proclaimed the essen‹ tial basis of democracy: the natural intellectual equality of man in the courts of reason. From this time onwards reason will steadily cease to be a special possession of special people (especially princes and priests), or something requiring discipline and training. It will become pretty much like common sense. It will be all the more effectively operative among

---

[1] *Monde* was commonly used for universe, and not merely the earth, at that time, thus making possible the pun: the beautiful universe = fashionable society.

ordinary, unspecialised minds, minds unencumbered by the lumber of the schools and the universities. The marquise will not be shy of ex, claiming triumphantly after five lessons: '*Je suis savante.*' Nor will M. Jourdain feel obliged to conceal his glee when he is told that he has been talking prose all his life. . . . These were not the things that Descartes was either wishing or expecting.

For Fontenelle, however, the really important thing was Descartes's cosmological treatise, *Le Monde*, his model of the physical universe as he built it up by reason from a few simple ideas. From a universe packed with matter (a plenum) into which God had put a certain fixed quantity of motion, the universe was a self-acting mechanism, a kind of celestial merry-go-round, involving no 'action at a distance', because in a plenum every particle is in direct operation upon its neighbour. God was not necessary to its action once he had created the matter and put in the motion. 'I cannot forgive Descartes,' said Pascal. 'In all his philosophy, he would have liked to dispense with God. But he could not help making God give a shove to set the world in motion. After that he has no further use for Him.' Motion in a plenum produces vortices, or whirlpools, all caught up in a larger one with the sun at its centre. This is the celebrated 'vorticist physics' which took the seventeenth century by storm. It was dramatic, it was simple, it was complete. It had all the qualities of a perfect work of art. Everything was accounted for. It left no loose ends. It answered all the questions. Its only defect was the fact that it was not true. It was an intellectual fabric which might have (indeed had) been worked out in the human brain without the aid of a telescope or of a single experiment. Almost at the moment when Fontenelle presented it as the basis of his celebrated book in 1686 Newton shattered it to pieces. *Principia Mathematica* came out in 1687.

Fontenelle remained quite impervious. As he hopped round at the ball with little Élisabeth Helvétius like one on his own *tourbillons* slowing down, his mind was still warm with Cartesian dreams. His last book, published when he was ninety-five, was called *La Théorie des tourbillons cartésiens*, which Dr Robert Shackleton has called a 'sustained, lucid ex, position of a moribund system'. It certainly is a wonderful example of the conservatism of science or of scientists. After all, Fontenelle had a vested interest in Cartesian science, indeed a life-interest. Nor need it be assumed that he was wholly an interested party. He genuinely believed that Newton was Descartes's inferior, that in the *Principia* he had re, introduced occult factors into sidereal physics, in fact that there was something occult about the theory of gravitation, or action at a distance.

Descartes had got rid of all such residual superstition in favour of a completely rational man‑made system. Here was Newton in his crabbed and crooked way allowing it all back again.

When it fell to Fontenelle's lot to deliver the *éloge* on Newton in 1727 the scientific world held its breath in expectation. 'In England', says Voltaire, 'we await the verdict of M. de Fontenelle as a solemn judgement in favour of the superiority of the English philosophy.' It turned out, however (to quote Dr Shackleton again), to be 'a masterpiece of elo‑ quence and tact', in which he gravely recounted Newton's doctrines of the vacuum and centripetal force, his theories of light and sound. He stated neatly the differences of Descartes and Newton as types of mind, the experimentalist and the *a priori* thinker, approaching the problems of science from opposite directions. But he made no attempt to judge between them as regards quality. They were both geniuses of the first rank, empire‑builders – 'born to hold sway over other minds and to build empires'. In remaining faithful to Descartes and in resisting Newton the French were not simply being patriots, but believed themselves to be upholding true scientific progress against retrogressive tendencies, and it was long before they ceased to suspect him of re‑introducing occultism into science. Nor, in the light of recent discoveries, is it possible to dis‑ miss their suspicions. The late Lord Keynes, having had a peep into the 'Black Box',[1] has called Newton

> the last of the magicians . . . the Babylonians and Sumerians, the last great mind which looked out on the visible and intellectual world with the same eyes as those who built our intellectual inheritance less than 10,000 years ago . . . the last wonder‑child to whom the Magi could do sincere and appropriate homage.

This man, the first and greatest of the modern age of scientists, who is supposed to have taught us to think on the lines of cold untinctured reason, was the child‑magician of the seventeenth century, born in the first half of it, at pains to conceal secret heresies and scholastic supersti‑ tions all his life; a Faust disguised in a peruke, a man to make Voltaire revolve in his grave, Fontenelle nod his head with a sage 'I told you so.'

Fontenelle published the *Entretiens* at the turning‑point of Louis XIV's career of aggression, when he crossed the Rhine and roused up

---

[1] See *Newton Tercentenary Celebrations*, 1946, to which he contributed an address which goes a long way to destroy the conventional view of Newton as the favourite son of the Age of Reason. The Black Box is the repository of Newton's mathematical papers in connection with Biblical exegesis.

against him the Grand Alliance of the Empire, Spain, Sweden and the Netherlands, a coalition soon to be completed by England, whose weight was thrown against the great Catholic monarchy by the Revolution of 1688 which brought a Protestant Dutch patriot to the throne. With the ravage of the Palatinate that followed – the wasting of some twenty miles of the Rhineland in a style which was to revive memories of the Huns and to poison German memories down to 1919 – *le grand monarque* became 'the most Christian Turk . . . the most Christian ravager of Christendom'. Against this background of fife-and-drum history, some-times glorious, often squalid, the small dark figure of young Bernard seems to vanish from our ken after the fashion of one of H. G. Wells's little men, Kipps or Mr Polly or Mr Lewisham, in the strong sunshine of Edwardian imperialism. It seems inapposite to imagine him going about the world of king-worship and intolerance. Yet there he was, *anima naturaliter moderna*, among the last enchantments of the Middle Ages, a mole burrowing busily under the gilded panoply of *le grand siècle*.

By the end of the century, when Fontenelle was still in his fifties, the Sun King seemed to have overcome all his enemies. He had tamed the nobility, expelled the Protestants, beaten down the Jansenists; Molière was dead, Racine was drying up; shortly, it seemed, there would be no more Pyrenees. Long ago he had founded the Académie Royale des Sciences and in 1697 Fontenelle became its perpetual Secretary. For more than forty years it was one of his principal duties to deliver the *éloges* at the deaths of men of science. He was thereby afforded a unique oppor-tunity to write the history of science while it was being made, to create year by year the heroic myth of science. He made capital use of these opportunities, providing each hero of science with a heroic life-pattern reminiscent of the pattern employed in the hagiography of sacred history. Not Migne's *Patrologia*, but Samuel Smiles's *Industrial Biography* is the nearest parallel in other ages. Fontenelle's work is but one item in a tremendous intellectual advance which was to cause Voltaire to bracket the Age of Louis XIV with that of Pericles and Virgil, the Italian Renaissance and the *Éclaircissement*. That old snob, the Duc de Saint-Simon, called it 'a long reign of the vile bourgeoisie!' And it is true that its artistic distinction was not primarily the fruit of the King's personal taste and intelligence. On the whole it was, as one man said, lucky for his reputation as a patron that he lived in the reign of Louis XIV. The Palace of Versailles was a memorial to the impoverishment of the mass of Frenchmen and to the suffering of the *fainéant* nobility

who lived there in mortal boredom. It has much of the character of a
mausoleum.

Le grand monarque himself took on some of the full character of a
bourgeois-gentilhomme in his later years, more especially after he married
his mistress, Madame de Maintenon, and devoted himself to 'the religion
of a parlour-maid'. By 1700 orthodoxy had ceased to count its victories.
Severity, piety, discipline were the order of the day. The royal *dévot* on
the throne had discovered the charms of penitence, the century had
disavowed the errors of its youth. Bossuet preached at its requiem in
dulcet tones, keeping his eye on every mousehole of dissent. The only
defect in his defensive system was the fact that the enemy he had hounded
down was not the real enemy after all. His thunderbolts were hurled at
a decoy. The real adversary was one he had never seen, the patient
worker in the laboratories where a new epoch of the human spirit was
being born, bringing about what Paul Hazard would one day call 'the
crisis of the European conscience'. It was in this, 'the open conspiracy'
of the seventeenth century, that Fontenelle had his part.

The earliest example of an intellectual phenomenon often reveals the
characteristics of the species at their furthest point of development. Thus
Fontenelle, spanning the century of the *Philosophes*, reveals all their
characteristics except their credulity and their social concern. He practised their craft of evasion, the treatment of dangerous matter with an
air of innocence; their ambiguity; their cult of amused speculation
instead of commitment. It was on the whole easy for him. As he himself
says:

> Happily one finds that in physical science the ideas are pleasing in
> themselves at the same time that they are satisfying to the reason,
> presenting to the imagination a spectacle which pleases it, almost as if
> it had been specially made for the purpose.

He established at a blow the full technique of popularisation by writing
for women, or (in his day) the lowest level of civilised intelligence. He
carried forward the *badinage*, the frivolity, of the *libertin* tradition, which
was to flourish in Montesquieu, Voltaire, Diderot and many more. He
was able to level his pseudo-learned chatter at the prevailing orthodoxy,
thereby promoting the relativity of morals. He taught the future how to
be serious without being solemn, that favourite stance of the greatest
of the twentieth-century *Philosophes*, Bernard Shaw. Finally, he would
assure his marquise: 'You are free *not* to believe anything I have told you',
adding that on the whole he hoped she would. He was perhaps the eighth
type of ambiguity, and the most profitable of them all.

Chapter Three

PARIS, 1715

FONTENELLE regarded Europe as exclusively the home of civilisation. 'Veritably,' he had told the marquise on their final evening, 'the longer I live the more I become convinced that there is a certain quality of genius which has never yet shown itself outside Europe.' When, a little later, he wrote his *Digression sur les anciens et les modernes*, he fixed Mount Atlas and the Baltic, Egypt and Sweden as the bounds of civilisation. He was inclined to think that science could not have any existence in the Torrid Zone or at the Poles. It was no good ever hoping to see great Laplandish or Negro authors. While Montesquieu satirised Europe at the hands of his Persian visitors in the celebrated *Lettres persanes*, and collected instructive information from every corner of the earth for his great work on *L'Esprit des lois*, he, like most people, took it for granted that the world meant Europe, Europe meant France, and France meant Paris.

In the eighteenth century all the capital cities of Europe were alike in the fact that they were beautiful. Canaletto has put much of their beauty on record, more especially that of London. Of course they stank, with their narrow cobbled streets, their ill-drained or undrained purlieus, their open garbage-gutters, as modern writers never fail to remind us in case we should be tempted to indulge in the great twentieth-century sin of nostalgia. But they were not yet smoke-grimed by industry nor brought to a halt and deafened by traffic. The Paris of the *Philosophes* was not, of course, as beautiful as that of the Impressionists or of Henry James, for the boulevard was introduced by modern dictators afraid of narrow streets and their suitability for barricades. Louis XIV, after his childhood fright at the Fronde, had built himself another town at Versailles. Not until the Revolution did the Parisians bring the King and Queen back to the old capital, the city of the Tuileries and the Louvre. The City of Light, in the physical sense, was largely the product of the nineteenth-century. The eighteenth-century *Cité des Lumières*, in the intellectual and cultural sense, was a town vibrating like a cerebral powerhouse. T. E. Lawrence, who said he was obliged to work at night when he was at Oxford because his brain was affected by the intellectual vibration around him in the daytime, would have had to move altogether. Only a work of art like René Clair's *Sous les toits de Paris*, made over again for the eighteenth century, could give a pictorial representation of its pulsating vitality. One imagines the very roofs and walls bulging.

It is said that no one is ever born in Paris, and that the Parisian is nearly always a displaced provincial. It is to a large extent true of the *Philosophes*. D'Alembert is said to have been found on the steps of the church of SaintJeanleRond, whence his Christian name. But his great colleague Denis Diderot was from Langres in Champagne, the town of the hundred weathervanes. Étienne Bonnot de Condillac came from Grenoble, the Comte de Buffon from Montbard in Burgundy, La Mettrie from StMalo, Condorcet from Picardy, the Baron d'Holbach from Speyer, beyond the frontier. Who else was born in Paris, if we leave out Voltaire, who, like Montesquieu, was something else than a *Philosophe*? A roadmap of France could be made to show the geographical distribution of the *Philosophes* like a spider's web, with Paris at the centre. Paris at that time was far more absorbent of the genius of France than London has ever been of the genius of England. Norwich, Birmingham, Bristol, all had a vigorous regional life as provincial capitals in the eighteenth century, while Paris was taking the vitality of France to herself. There the *illuminati* lived in a variety of habitations, some in medieval garrets at the top of tall buildings like the wynds of Edinburgh, some in *appartements*, or suites of rooms in an *hôtel* or mansion, like the lodgings of students in a college or barristers in their chambers in the inns of court. The housefront of a garretdwelling would be a ramshackle plasterfaced survival from the Middle Ages. The front of the *hôtel* would be square, *carré*, with mansards, possibly built in the reign of Henri Quatre. Since Louis XIV's time, there were lights everywhere, five thousand lamps burning every night, and the same king had completely paved the city and established guards, mounted and on foot, to secure the safety of citizens, a condition of things hardly dreamt of in other urban centres.

Like Frenchmen in all ages, the Parisians lived at home for only a small part of each day, going out to their meals at cafés and restaurants, and (more especially the intelligentsia) spending most evenings in attendance at the salons of great ladies, and ladies less great. A very considerable portion of one's time was given to social intercourse, which in France meant conversation. As Carlyle once said, only towards the small hours did the tide of French speech withdraw slightly to the ebb.

Conversation ranged from sheer badinage to sustained discussion of the latest ideas, and a great deal of it combined the two. Men talked their books while writing them. Claude-Adrien Helvétius (1715–71), little Élisabeth's father, and old Fontenelle's young friend, was notorious for his tactical withdrawals to the nearest alcove with a notebook when something apposite struck him in the conversation. He was, they said, writing his masterpiece. Many of the second-rate books of the age were really the product of multiple collaboration of this kind. It was the tone of the salons, those everlasting talking-shops, which helps to account for the lightness and grace of the style in which most of the work of the *Philosophes* was written. Everything had to be reduced to the lightness of puff-pastry if it was to be tossed about in a salon. No lady-hostess would tolerate the difficult, the complicated, *la sèche*. An idea might not be amusing in itself, but it had to be *made* amusing. Otherwise *cela ne marche pas*, and was best forgotten. Sometimes it was, no doubt, fatiguing. Horace Walpole thought much of the salon-life was a sheer bore and a waste of time. But he was not very good at French of the rapid conversa-tional sort.

The literary forms natural to this type of society were of course con-versational in character: the *entretiens*, or dialogue, or colloquy; the *conte*, which was really a story; the *lettres*; the *essai*. If a man wrote a *traité*, he was not a *Philosophe* but a philosopher, though of course some authors of long and learned works managed to get away with a reputation for *légèreté*, by dividing a big book into a large number of short chapters, which is what Montesquieu did with *De l'esprit des lois*, a work of several hundred chapters, one of which is less than three lines and another of more than ten pages. But then, as Madame du Deffand said, he was really writing '*L'esprit sur les lois*'. Fontenelle knew very well what he was doing in his *Entretiens*. 'I have wished to treat of philosophy in an unphilosophical way', he said in his preface. He had not made it any more difficult for his lady readers than Madame de La Fayette's novel, *La Princesse de Clèves*. It was the kind of thing that Macaulay hoped to do for history, to replace for an hour the latest novel on the young lady's dressing-table. The affiliation of such a work with the life of the salon may be seen from the author's prefatory apology for digressions. He had only adopted 'the natural freedom of conversation'.

As a social phenomenon, the salon, dominated by *légèreté* favoured by the ladies and shunning specialisation, concerned predominantly with the *bel esprit* of literary men and women, went back to the early years of the seventeenth century. It may be said to have sprung from

B

the *chambre bleu* of the Marquise de Rambouillet. The first and most famous of the salon hostesses, however, was Madeleine de Scudéry (1607–1701) in the age of the Fronde at the middle of the century. These early salons were really versions of the 'courts of love' of the later Middle Ages, concerned less with debate than with a highly mannered cult of court-ship. Molière satirised them in his first Parisian play, *Les Précieuses ridicules* (1659). In his *Les Femmes savantes* (1672) he developed it into a full-scale satire of pseudo-literature and pseudo-learning in general. By the eighteenth century, however, the Paris salon had developed into the social phenomenon remembered under the names of such celebrated hostesses as Madame Geoffrin and Madame du Deffand, whose salons were the haunts of the literati and the *beaux esprits*. The illuminati, especially the *Philosophes*, tended to frequent circles in which the con-versation was more scientific and specialised, such as the society of *L'Entresol* which met above Madame Pompadour's apartment at Ver-sailles. Here Dr Quesnay and the Physiocrats congregated. Turgot himself, Diderot, d'Alembert and Helvétius were frequently there, whereas Diderot was deliberately excluded from Madame de Geoffrin's. Madame Helvétius's salon in the Rue Sainte-Anne, or later out at Auteuil, was less favoured by *les Philosophes* than was that of the Baron d'Holbach (known as "the Synagogue d'Holbach", or *le café de l'Europe*). The beautiful Madame Helvétius, it was said, tended to break up the conversation by attaching the most interesting man of the evening to her-self, whereas Madame d'Holbach was less intrusive and, as Marmontel puts it, 'We were no longer tied to a woman's apron-strings.' The salons of the last decades before the Revolution tended to be different in tone from the famous social centres of the great ladies, more masculine, more serious, more adventurous, dominated by the interests of men who in-tended to change the world rather than to gossip about it and the latest fashion in ideas. They were doubtless more middle-class, and the Syna-gogue d'Holbach tended to show many traces of English influence, with the occasional presence of such visitors as the Rev. Laurence Sterne, John Wilkes and Lord Shelburne.

The presence of a number of such conversational centres dominated by the ease and clarity of the French language, coining phrases which passed from tongue to tongue throughout a 'talking-shop' of some half a million highly vocal people, was an enormous auxiliary to the influence of the written word. Fontenelle's marquise was not alone when she ex-claimed with delight: *'Je suis savante!'* To be *savante* was the fashion, and to its social spread there was literally no limit. 'Everybody wants to be a philosopher,' complained the Abbé Nonotte, author of the *Dictionnaire philosophique de la religion* (1774), 'to reason, to judge and to decide about everything in a philosophical manner.' The Marquis d'Argens once said that within fifteen years of the publication of Descartes's *Discours* in French ladies were reasoning better than three-quarters of the theolo-gians. Descartes's paternity of the *Philosophes* is illustrated by the title of his unfinished dialogue between Eudoxe and Mentor: *Recherche de la vérité par la lumière naturelle*, which goes on to announce that it simply decides the opinions which should be held by an honest man without the assistance of either religion or philosophy. He boasts of using the language of polite conversation for this purpose. Is it to be wondered at that Coleridge proclaimed, a century later, that the very ladies and hair-dressers of Paris were become fluent Encyclopedists? It was perhaps remarkable to an Englishman who knew little of France and the French, but to anyone possessed of any experience of the part played by women in French society it was a commonplace.

When the Abbé Mercier wrote his book about Paris in 1781 he called it 'The Waiting City' – waiting presumably for the Revolution.[1] That the city was to be the scene of revolution was hidden from those who lived and wrote and talked so brilliantly in the age of the *Philosophes*. Not Paris but London was the more likely home of insurrection. Parisians were rather inclined to suppose that nothing very upsetting could happen to a society of such well-instructed and intelligent people. While it would be absurd to suppose that the Revolution, when it came, was like a bolt from a blue sky, it would be no less absurd to imagine that people sup-posed themselves to be living on the slopes of a volcano. People had their premonitions, but they would appear to have felt a certain assurance that they would, in the event, have things well under control. It was an age of reform, an age of despotism but of enlightened despotism, from Russia to Spain, from Denmark to Naples. The King of France was himself attempting reform in his somewhat spineless way, and reform was the enemy of revolution. When reform actually turned into revolu-tion, it was, as Albert Schweitzer was to say, 'a fall of snow on blossoming trees'.

How to prevent the catastrophe? The French middle class had its ideas. Under the impact of 'enlightenment', especially at the hands of that great 'book of the words' for a power-hungry middle class, the Encyclopedia, it was deeply conscious of its own potentialities as the

---

[1] Louis-Sébastien Mercier (1744–1814) wrote the first two volumes in 1781 and com-pleted it in twelve volumes in 1788.

governing class of France. The bourgeoisie after Descartes had been pleased to discover that reason 'was indistinguishable from *le bon sens*'. As Professor Butterfield puts it: there were 'sections of the French intelligentsia who could claim to understand the idea of the state better than the king himself'. These were the people who had been taught over a course of years by the *Philosophes*. It was the historical function of the *Philosophes*, from Fontenelle to Diderot, to translate the science, the philosophy and the mathematical genius of the seventeenth century into a new outlook upon politics and society. This was rapidly being effected by the second half of the eighteenth century. Men had been educated in *une nouvelle façon commune de penser*. This, more than anything else, signalised the birth of modern history. In comparison, the actual Revolution which took place in France in 1789, was secondary, some would have said in large part irrelevant. For history is what happens in men's heads.

Chapter Four

VOLTAIRE AND NEWTON

WHEN Voltaire wrote his *conte*, *Micromégas*, in 1752, he described
Fontenelle as 'a very witty man who indeed never invented anything but
who gave a very good account of the inventions of others'. '*Le Secrétaire*'
is made to use a very gay and flowery style, and, when asked why, he
replies 'to please you'. Voltaire also admitted that the *Entretiens* was 'a
book unique of its kind'. This was in 1740 when he was writing his great
Essai sur les mœurs. Two years earlier, in writing to Maupertuis, the
scientist-philosopher of whom he made much fun in *Micromégas*, he
professed to see the mind of France in great ferment: 'the names of
Descartes and Newton seem to be the rallying-cries of two parties'.
Voltaire had chosen his party at least as early as 1726 when he was in
England. A Frenchman arriving in London, he said, found philosophical
matters and all else very different from what they were in Paris. At Paris
the heavens were full of *tourbillons*. At London they were clean-swept
and empty. You had exchanged *le monde plein* for *le monde vide*. And it
was nothing to do with the weather.

There was something immensely refreshing about coming to England
after the War of the Spanish Succession. For years past the country had
been *terra incognita*. Few Frenchmen could speak or read English, and
most were innocent of knowledge of the intellectual revolution which
had happened there since the restoration of the monarchy in 1660. Of
course it was well known that England had a Royal Society, but, as
Voltaire said, 'it is not so well run as ours', chiefly because it was older.
Pierre Coste's translation of Locke's great *Essay*, which was to become
the Bible of the Enlightenment, did not appear until 1700. Madame du
Châtelet, while eulogising Coste for his translation, could still ask how
many of those Frenchmen who had learnt English in order to read Locke
had understood him? It was, in fact, her lover who did most to bring
England and the 'English Philosophy' to the French. Voltaire's *Lettres
philosophiques* had as its sub-title *Lettres anglaises*. He had gone to England,
self-exiled after a stay in the Bastille, in 1726. He stayed in England for

two years – though some said he was spiritually there for the rest of his life. In 1738 he published his *Éléments de la philosophie de Newton*.

What Voltaire especially praised about both Locke and Newton was their *modestie*. Instead of boasting like the followers of Descartes 'Give me matter and motion, and I will make a world',[1] they confessed that they did not understand the final cause of things. This was especially true of Sir Isaac Newton, who said that the 'cause of causes' was hidden in the bosom of the Deity, and that he had composed his *Principia Mathematica* in the hope that it 'might work with considering men for the belief of a deity'. As Diderot was to ask: 'Who are we to explain the ends of nature?' As for Locke, his *Essay on the Human Understanding* was in effect an essay on the *limits* of the understanding. Fontenelle had ascribed to Newton 'a gentle character' which 'naturally leads to modesty'. It was not in the least surprising that such a man believed in revelation and that the book most often in his hands was the Bible. Voltaire summed up Locke's modesty in the words: 'Plenty of reasoners have given us the story of the mind; at last a wise man has arrived to give us its *history*.' Both had started from observed facts in order to arrive at principles, which was the way Englishmen generally proceeded. It was perhaps the difference between the mental habits of the two peoples. 'We are prone to eschew the general,' Austen Chamberlain once said, while M. Painlevé's contribution to the same debate was: 'The Latin mentality delights in starting from abstract principles and passing from generalities to details; the Anglo-Saxon mentality, on the other hand, prefers to proceed from individual concrete cases to generalisations.' They were seeking to explain the divergent English and French attitudes to the Geneva Protocol of 1925, the white hope in that year of preserving international peace.

Fontenelle was wholly French. Voltaire, like Karl Marx, was an Englishman by adoption. It was this, along with his genius, that preserved him from becoming a *Philosophe*. Like Hamlet to Horatio, he would protest: There are more things in Heaven and Earth than are dreamt of in our philosophy. He satirised the race in *Micromégas*. He was only recruited for their Encyclopedia, by the persuasions of d'Alembert, when it reached the fifth volume, and even then he did little more than lend to it the cachet of his invaluable name; though it is true that he contributed the article on 'FORNICATION', which opens with the unimpeachably true statement that according to the Jesuit *Journal de Trévoux* 'this is a term in theology'. After all, he had his own *Dictionnaire philosophique* (1764).

[1] The remark was attributed by Voltaire to Descartes himself.

He was never less than a deist and found the atheism and materialism of the *Philosophes* as repulsive as the dogmatism of the Church. Nor was he ever a democrat, having a horror of the *canaille* and a lifelong faith in enlightened despotism.

Did it matter, apart from patriotic sentiment, whose side the *Philoso, phes* were on, Descartes's or Newton's? Was it simply an aesthetic choice whether you preferred the heavens full of *tourbillons* or under the pull of gravity? In fact the choice went far beyond either patriotism or aesthetics. It was a matter of knowing all and everything with Descartes, or resting content with half,knowledge[1] after the modest style of the great Englishman, and leaving something to God. The former would seem to consort best with the passion for comprehensiveness of the men who made the great Encyclopedia. They really did believe they had taken everything into account. D'Alembert, writing of the intellectual fertility of the mid,century, put it into so many words:

> Thus, from the principles of the secular sciences to the foundations of religious revelation, from metaphysics to matters of taste, from music to morals . . . everything has been discussed and analysed, or at least mentioned.

This was very much in the tradition of Descartes who, when he came to the one,hundred,and,ninety,ninth of his Principles of Philosophy, wrote: 'there is no phenomenon of nature which has not been dealt with in this treatise'. Human vanity seeks after completeness or comprehensiveness. Diderot himself concluded the eleventh *Pensée* in his *Interprétation de la nature* that, in tackling nature: 'no one fact can be regarded as completely independent of the rest; without the notion of the totality of nature, there can be no philosophy'. Mere empiricism, after the manner of Newton, can reveal only a fragmentary order whose primary and genera, tive principles remain mysterious, thus leaving a loophole for the one thing the *Philosophes* were determined to exclude – the occult, the final cause, even God himself. The Newtonian *modestie* in the face of nature was unsatisfactory; the Cartesian *orgueil* in grasping the totality of things was indispensable.

It is, therefore, only in a purely temporal sense that Fontenelle's successor is to be discovered in Voltaire, the devout Newtonian. His truest successor in all senses is rather Bayle the sceptic. Of course it is always unwise to imagine a strict heredity in ideas. As Coleridge said, that there are two kinds of heads in the world of literature, springs and tanks. Voltaire was a spring. Fontenelle and Bayle were both tanks,

[1] Like Keats's poet with his 'negative capability'.

'habituated to receiving only'. Like everybody else, Voltaire was also in many respects a receiver, and like every figure of the Enlightenment he received a great deal from Pierre Bayle. Bayle was the keeper of the great quarry from which eighteenth-century critics of unreason cut their stones. Perhaps it was less a quarry than a powder-magazine or an armoury. Much of the powder and shot fired at prejudice, intolerance and unreason were taken from Bayle's *Dictionnaire historique et critique* which served, in its limited fashion, as a kind of one-man Encyclopedia of the seventeenth century. Bayle was not really a *Philosophe*. He was the complete sceptic. Certain things which the *Philosophes* practised to perfection they learnt from Bayle's tactics in composing his dictionary, notably the tactics of evasion, or how to say dangerous things with the poker-face of a simple scholar, and how to entertain the reader by a learned salaciousness, much after the tradition of the *libertin* writers of earlier years.

Bayle lived from 1647 to 1706, almost contemporary with Fontenelle, though for half a century less. The comparative brevity of his life is perfectly understandable in view of his perilous course and his weevil-like labours. He was born at Carla, under the Pyrenees, son of a Protest-ant pastor. Somewhat after the style of Gibbon, he was converted to the Roman Church, and after removing to the University of Geneva he renounced it, to suffer the peculiar malice of priests towards a 'lapsed Catholic'. He had a dual experience of intolerance, from Catholics and Calvinists alike. When he was Professor of Theology at Sedan (1675–81) it was closed down as part of Louis XIV's anti-Huguenot campaign, and after that he was Professor of History and Philosophy at Rotterdam until the Dutch Calvinists secured his dismissal in 1693. He lived in Rotterdam, however, for the rest of his life, veritably at 'the cross-roads of Europe', in the track of *émigrés* eluding persecution. It was an admir-able point at which to edit the periodical *Nouvelles de la république des lettres*, which after 1684 served as the exchange and mart of liberal ideas and a review, predecessor of the literary and philosophical exchanges of the Enlightenment. In these early years at Rotterdam he published his *Pensées sur la comète*, that flaming apparition in the heavens which created great perturbation in 1680. He described the comet as one of 'the ordinary works of nature which, without regard to the happiness of mankind, are transported from one part of the heavens to another by virtue of the general laws of nature'. The essay served, as so often with Bayle, as cover for an attack on general superstition, and on belief in miracles. It went further, which was also typical, in turning an innocent

subject into a vehicle for the defence of the morals of atheists. He propounded his view that there was no necessary connection between a man's
morals and his religion. Like his disciple, David Hume, he appears to
have thought that 'it required a great goodness of disposition to with-
stand the baneful effects of Christianity', and that the morality of all
religions was on the whole bad. Thus in his first book Bayle employed
the method that was to serve him all his life, and especially in the pro-
motion of scepticism, by the serious treatment of an innocuous subject.

The remainder of Bayle's work before he devoted himself to the great
dictionary was concerned with two subjects which were to become
principal concerns of Voltaire: religious toleration and the writing of
history. In his bitter tract *The Character of France entirely Catholic* (1685)
and his *Commentaire philosophique sur les paroles de Jésus-Christ:
'Contrains-les d'entrer'* (1686) he attacks the abominable nature of forcible
conversion as it was practised in the France of Louis XIV, with special
reference to the sophistries of St Augustine in the defence of persecution.
On the writing of history he was concerned with answering Maimbourg's
Histoire du calvinisme (1682), anticipating Voltaire's thesis that Jesuits
and Calvinists alike were disqualified from writing history because by
reason of prejudice they were incapable of being truthful. 'Writing
history is no suitable function for a priest; it is a function that requires
objectivity in everything, and a priest can be objective about nothing.'
It is often said that the *Philosophes* lacked history. In fact they made
excellent use of it, and in doing so they learnt their lessons from Bayle.
Pierre Bayle's *Dictionnaire historique et critique* had its first edition in 1697
at Rotterdam. By 1750 it had gone through nine editions in France, three
in England and one in Germany. There were in addition many abridged
editions. The work has been called the most popular book in the eighteenth century. No massive tome on a gentleman's bookshelf or in a
college library ever bore so forbidding an external aspect or contained
in its voluminous pages so entertaining, albeit poisonous, an assortment
of learned articles. More than two centuries after the work appeared, a
selection has been made by two American scholars, E. A. Beller and
M. du P. Lee, and published by the University of Princeton (1952),
which permits the twentieth-century reader to sample some of the more
delightful items of the dictionary without searching the many double
columns of painful black print. For Bayle was intent on hiding his best
things in the small type of footnotes and under unlikely headings. His
favourite technique was to begin with a grave and formal statement of a
perfectly orthodox kind, generally brief, and then to proceed to several

B 2

columns of small print, like the reverse of an insurance policy. These columns are sometimes scandalous or indecent, always argumentative, fulfilling both the 'critical' and the 'historical' pretensions of the work.

Sometimes, however, he will go in for straightfaced absurdity from the beginning, delivering himself of statements that can be read with equal relish by both the sceptical and the devout. ADAM, for instance, is discussed in biographical terms as the first historical man. We are told his physical dimensions, his extensive knowledge, even his place of burial. There are, too, learned disputes about procreation to follow. DAVID, again, is given full historical treatment like any other king, ancient or modern. He comes out of it badly, so that 'the man after God's own heart' serves as a scathing commentary upon the Divine good taste. The irreverence of dealing with the figures of sacred history on precisely the same footing as all others got Bayle into serious trouble, but by it he earned the title of the founder of the Biblical criticism which was to flourish with Voltaire. The Saints came off even worse than the Old Testament rulers. Serious consideration is given to the theory that St Bernard was a dog ('the watch-dog of the Faith') and St Augustine a wine-bibber. Whenever he has the chance to discuss rival faiths he manages to satirise the Christians. The article on 'MANICHEE' is perhaps the most important here. He calls Manicheanism 'an abominable heresy', though he gives it the victory in important points in its contest with Catholic Christianity. The Roman Church, he contends, should be profoundly grateful that St Augustine changed sides, for with the strength of the Manichean argument and the genius of St Augustine to defend it, it must have won an everlasting victory. His ingenious propositions on the intellectual impressiveness of the Manichean argument were held abominable by the Walloon Church, so that he was obliged to take evasive physical action, though he never formally withdrew his opinions. Nothing is so important in the *Philosophes'* debt to Bayle as his light-hearted irreverence, and his liberation of history from dogmatic control. He achieved for historical writing what Galileo achieved for natural science. History was never again to be respected if it was based on dogmatically 'given' authority of Church, or Bible, or anything else. There was to be no more special treatment for 'sacred' subject matter. He provided a sharp instrument for isolating the kernel of historical truth from the accumulated husk and rind of fable and legend. He set modern standards of historical enquiry.

This is where Bayle's achievement ends; a philosophy of history was quite outside his province, perhaps beyond his powers. But by forging the weapons for the emancipation of historical thinking, and by the ethical standards of his historical science, he made possible the construc‹ tive work of the future. What interests him is the process of acquiring fact. Fact with Bayle is not the starting‹point but the goal. And his genius lies not in the discovering of the truth but in the discovery of the false. His dictionary was, by his own profession, a dictionary of correc‹ tions: to correct the *Grand Dictionnaire historique* of Moreri (1674), a work of Catholic bias and of many errors. Most of all, he had what Oakeshott calls the 'hydroptic thirst' of the *Philosophe* for knowledge, all knowledge, without discrimination. The *Dictionnaire historique et critique* is an aggregate of details, a heap of ruins, a flood of knowledge, without either inner order or philosophical method. In other words, a quarry, an armoury, a magnificent subject for looting: looting which went on for the hundred years called the Enlightenment.

Another and more disparate source of the material of the *Philosophes* is the 'clandestine literature' which circulated in France during the first half of the eighteenth century, the period of strict literary censorship. The notion that the despotism of the French monarchy of the *ancien régime* ever effectively suppressed 'dangerous thoughts' requires a great deal of modification. The celebrated remark of La Bruyère, which he made in 1688, that 'A man born Christian and French finds that he is restricted in satire; the great subjects are forbidden him', is more of a reproach than a statement of fact. Only by paying attention to the amount of clandestine literature of the early eighteenth century is it possible to attain a proper perspective with regard to the great efflux of unorthodox (often materialist) writings which went into print when the censorship was relaxed in the time of Malesherbes at the mid‹century mark. To make sense of the later situation it must be understood that the clandestine works which have been traced[1] represented only a ninth part of an iceberg. The submerged bulk is hardly likely to be discovered by the very nature of things. Indeed, it is more than possible that the clandestinity of the literature was some measure of its popularity. After all there was no likelihood of the man in the street (or the fields) reading such works even had they been openly obtainable.

Printing could be prevented. Writing could not, nor the circulation of manuscript among friends. What actually happened was a return to the conditions that prevailed before the invention of printing. For a time, the most cultivated society in Europe returned to the Middle Ages.

[1] Notably by Professor I. O. Wade in his *Clandestine Organisation and Diffusion of Philosophic Ideas in France, 1700–1750* (Princeton, 1938).

There were circles and syndicates of producers which engaged private copyists, like that of the Comte de Boulainvilliers (1658–1722) or the Duc de Noailles. The 'con*men*' for such wares were pedlars, café‹ keepers, *colporteurs* like Voltaire's little hunchback who carried copies of Jean Meslier's *Testament* in his mantle in the 1740s. The recipients were noblemen, bishops, abbés, the *Philosophes* themselves. If a copyist or a distributor were caught he frequently professed only to have translated the material discovered among the effects of a deceased writer. In any case, the accused generally recanted freely before the ecclesiastical authorities with promises to sin no more, promises which were immedi‹ ately broken. If the Bastille were prescribed, detention was generally brief and conditions were scarcely rigorous. The traffic afforded a number of sporting features calculated to relieve the monotony of life under despotism. Provincial centres of the contraband trade were Rouen, Châlons‹sur‹Marne, Aix and Fécamp. Single copies have been discovered at Bordeaux and Morlaix, several at Rheims and Auxerre, Rochefort and Vire. Even today, Professor Wade has discovered, there are nearly 400 extant copies of 102 works. Clergy and members of the Parlements pro‹ vided a good market, and it is difficult to imagine anyone having to go short of any work he was intent on reading. The France of the *ancien régime* died principally of inefficiency.

And ridicule. As early as 1721 a great roar of laughter went up on the publication of *Lettres persanes*, a satire on church and state by a nobleman of Gascony, the Baron de la Brède et de Montesquieu. In 160 letters purporting to pass between Persian visitors travelling in Europe, and especially in France, ridicule was openly levelled at just those features of the establishment which Voltaire was concerned to subject to the criti‹ cism of contrast in his *Lettres anglaises*. Between them, these two loosened the crumbling mortar of the old order with the points of a couple of extremely sharp pens. No more than Voltaire was Montesquieu a *Philosophe* in the sectarian sense. His masterpiece, *De l'esprit des lois* (1748), more than a quarter of a century later, was to establish him fairly above the propagandists of reason, as Voltaire's great historical work, *L'Essai sur les mœurs*, set him fairly in the history of historical writing. Montesquieu certainly shared the passion of the *collectionneur* for the acquisition of information from every quarter of the globe, but it was hardly the 'hydroptic thirst' of the *Philosophes*. He began by establishing principles: 'I established principles and saw particular cases conform to them as if automatically . . . When I discovered those principles, every‹ thing I was seeking came to me . . .' Which André Gide calls 'an amazing declaration', insisting that Montesquieu only reached that satisfactory result 'because he was seeking only what he had found in advance. Frightful limitation!' Whatever the truth about his empiricism, he certainly escaped the undiscriminating fact-hunting passion of the *Philosophe*. At the same time, he rejected their credulity, 'I who don't believe that too much reason is desirable, and that men are generally more prone to take a moderate position than an extreme one.'

Both Voltaire and Montesquieu knew and valued England and English things because they valued liberty and moderate government. Voltaire might have subscribed his *Lettres philosophiques* with the sub-title 'England an Example to France', though the very nature of Montes-quieu's thesis would prevent him from recommending one country to copy another. Voltaire, however, surveying the prosperous prospects of the people who had brought Louis XIV to his knees, put two and two together and made at least five. The English were the successful people, he decided, because they were free. They had a limited monarchy, numerous religious sects, and an independent judiciary. They were a people who buried Newton like a king. Montesquieu taught Europe in general to admire the English Constitution. Between them the two men delivered to the *Philosophes* their English inheritance, Newtonian science, Lockeian psychology, religious toleration, the rule of law. Most of them, however, retained a taste for enlightened despotism, they made a new dogmatism of their unbelief, and they turned Locke's psychology into what John Mill once called 'the shallowest set of doctrines which perhaps were ever passed off upon a cultivated age as a complete physiological system'.

Chapter Five

CONDILLAC AND LOCKE

JOHN LOCKE has always been famous in his own country for his second *Treatise on Government*, a work which was published so promptly after the Glorious Revolution of 1688 that it was for long regarded as having been written as its apology or justification. It was neither, though it might well have been, for it made the principle of limited monarchy philo‚ sophically secure. Government was declared to be for the protection of property and the right of the subject to change his government in the event of government's violation of natural rights, the chief of which was the right of the subject to possess his property in peace and security. These, it might be readily assumed, were the very principles to attract people living under despotism, like most of the peoples of eighteenth‚ century Europe, and more especially the French.

The second *Treatise on Government*, however, was not the work which chiefly attracted the French. The name of Locke meant rather his great *Essay Concerning the Human Understanding* which came out in the same year and has been called 'the Bible of the Enlightenment'. This work opens with the dismissal of the theory of innate ideas and the assertion that all our ideas are derived from our senses. The mind is described as a *tabula rasa*, a blank sheet, on which sensual experience writes: a highly attractive theory for reformers of all kinds, and especially penal re‚ formers, for it could now be assumed that a man does wrong not because of inherent depravity but because the wrong things have been written by life upon his *tabula rasa*. In other words, as one of Locke's critics was to put it, 'vice is the effect of error and the offspring of surrounding circum‚ stances, the object therefore of condolence not of anger'.[1] Environment is what makes criminals, and, as men were soon to say, '*L'éducation peut tout*'. A large part of eighteenth‚century optimism about the possibility of remaking man by remaking his environment was to spring from a rather naïve reading of John Locke's celebrated *Essay*, Pierre Coste's French translation of which (with the author's collaboration) was avail‚

[1] Coleridge, *Conciones ad Populum* (1795).

able in Locke's lifetime. It is difficult to imagine a philosophical doctrine more acceptable to a people looking for a gospel of reform.

There is a certain rather spurious simplicity about Locke's picture of the human understanding. He takes it for granted that it can be resolved into ideas as a building can be resolved into building-materials, which is an excellent example of what Alfred North Whitehead called 'misplaced concreteness'. Ideas come into the mind from sense experience, whether in the form of sensations or reflections, rather as images come into a box-camera through its lens. Locke is quite prepared to use such analogies:

> For methinks the understanding is not much unlike a closet wholly shut from the light, with only some little opening left to let in external, visible resemblances or ideas of things without: would the pictures coming into such a dark room but stay there, and lie so orderly as to be found upon occasion, it would very much resemble the understanding of man, in reference to all objects of sight, and the ideas of them.

It is, however, typical of John Locke in his modesty to add: 'these are my guesses'. The disciples were less cautious. They often preferred to deal in certainties. They were inclined to assume that the understanding is merely passive, a storehouse for simple ideas reaching it from sense-impressions, what Coleridge called 'a lazy looker-on' at the external world. Locke himself insists that the mind has the power to repeat and compare and unite simple ideas in infinite variety, thus forming complex ideas: a power of synthesis, a play of activity, which alone can explain the highest faculties of the mind.

The greatest of Locke's French disciples was Étienne Bonnot de Condillac. Born at Grenoble in 1715, he was the youngest son of the Vicomte de Mably, who belonged to the *noblesse de robe*. The boy was of fragile physique and weak eyesight, so that he developed late, being unable to read at the age of twelve. Jean-Jacques Rousseau, who was for a time tutor in the de Mably household, records that Étienne was thought to be '*un esprit borné*', although when the backward boy grew into the distinguished man he added: 'That excellent brain matured silently.' He went to the Jesuit college at Lyons, and then to the seminary of Saint-Sulpice at Paris and to the Sorbonne. His theological studies were always somewhat perfunctory, for he was principally interested in science and natural philosophy. He soon joined the great stage-army of the eighteenth-century clergy which consisted of *abbés*, men entitled to be addressed as 'Reverend Sir' but neither professed to all the vows nor necessarily beneficed. The Abbé Condillac is recorded as having said only one Mass after his ordination. As one of the de Mably family he plunged into the high society of the Paris of his time, having a particular fondness for salons rather than churches. Like the great René Descartes a century earlier, he embarked on a fervid course of re-education, for, as he says in his *Cours d'études*, 'When we leave school we have to forget the trivial stuff we have been taught, and to learn useful things that they never dreamt of teaching us.' Above all, he versed himself in 'the English philosophy', studying Pierre Coste's translation of Locke's *Essay*, the Latin of Newton's *Principia* and the French of Voltaire's *Éléments de la philosophie de Newton*. Later he was to equip himself at the English fountainhead in the works of Bacon.

In Paris, Condillac associated with Diderot and d'Alembert, not to mention his old acquaintance Rousseau. 'As we all lived in widely different quarters,' Rousseau was to write in his *Confessions*, 'the three of us met once a week at the Palais-Royal and went to dine together at the Panier-Fleuri.' At this time, the Abbé was writing his first book, *L'Essai sur l'origine des connaissances humaines*, for which Rousseau claims to have got him a hundred crowns. This was in 1746, and the essay proved to be the first of a whole succession of works which were to occupy a high place in the history of psychology and even in the twentieth century are to be respected as pioneer contributions to the subject. He was captivated by John Locke's study of the human understanding, conducted as it was independently of all metaphysics and strictly bounded by experience. He set himself to carry it on with greater rigour, or, as he hoped, to make himself 'the Newton of psychology'. Newton was his model of a career and of fame. With Locke's analytical description of the understanding, and Newton's devotion to a single principle which explains the whole of nature, he would devote his life to the uncompleted task of Locke. At the opening of his first work, whose title almost precisely reproduces the title of Locke's *Essay concerning Human Understanding*, he at once declared his intention, which was not to discover the nature of the human mind but to understand its operations. He sets out with an exposition of Locke's principle that experience is the origin of all our ideas, and proceeds to an exposition of the faculties of the understanding: perception, attention, memory, imagination, etc. He then departs from Locke, being unwilling to explain reflection, that complex and even creative faculty, by talking of some mysterious 'initiative' on the part of the mind. Instead, he has recourse to speech, that unique prerogative of the human race, which is itself a product of the elementary faculties of the mind. Speech, he decided, was capable of accounting for the transposition of sensation into reflection. Instead of some mysterious inner spiritual activity, innate in the mind, which produces complex ideas from simple (sense-produced) ideas in association, Condillac advanced the view that language (first simple signs and then articulate speech) gave birth to reflection. Thanks to language, man ceased to be the sport of the successive impressions which things made on his mind and became 'master of what he was thinking'.

This was a new and profound thesis. It was the product of Condillac's attachment to a logical rigour which Locke lacked. It supplied a doctrinal unity to his philosophy of mind which would have been disrupted by the admission of any such hypothesis as some mysterious inner activating initiative in the mind. Condillac's originality lies in this: he had perceived in man's use of signs and words not simply a secondary function of the mind but the cause of its most complex operations. He had thereby advanced beyond Locke in the direction of consistency, logic and unity of doctrine. He worked out a number of views of the philosophy of language which twentieth-century philosophers have reached afresh and generally without knowledge of his pioneer work in their field.

Le Traité des sensations, however, which appeared six years later, was – and is – Condillac's most famous work. Its best-known feature is Condillac's expository use of a statue, or a human being with a marble exterior impervious to external influences, whose sense-organs are brought one by one into activity. He wished to study each sense in turn, and the way in which they modify each other by their interrelationship. He describes how the statue progressively comes to life and acquires an increasingly rich spiritual content because the individual senses engrave their special content on the marble. He tries to show that the continuous series of 'impressions' and the temporal order in which they are produced are sufficient to build up the totality of psychological experience and to produce it in all its wealth and subtle shadings.[1]

The employment of the statue 'model' readily lent itself to ridicule, though in fact it soon gives way to the more natural model of a human being whose faculties are all intact and whose sense-organs have not yet functioned. We see them coming into action one by one, and affecting each other. Condillac was fully aware that the statue idea would appear to the reader as nothing but a foolish fantasy, and he begs for his patience (and perhaps a certain amount of credulity) in a prefatory note entitled 'Advice of some importance to the Reader'. He was not amusing

[1] See Ernst Cassirer's *Philosophy of the Enlightenment*, 24-5.

himself, or his readers, with the popular Pygmalion myth of a statue which miraculously evolves life and sensibility, a legend which enjoyed great popularity in the literature of the Age of Reason, the age of ingenious mechanical toys like *serinettes* or 'bird‹organs', and of Vaucan‹ son's clockwork duck and flute‹player. It was the age when Diderot could say that the only difference between a man and a 'bird‹organ' was a difference of organisation, and that human beings were like clavi‹ chords possessed of greater sensitivity, and Condillac was writing only two years after the publication of La Mettrie's *L'Homme machine* with its thesis that monkeys could become men if they only had a few more, and more complicated, 'works'. The genesis of Frankenstein was already evident. This kind of thing did not particularly interest the Abbé Condillac. He was simply making expository use of an image that had quite other uses in his age. He was developing the ideas of John Locke's *Essay Concerning the Human Understanding* with a rigour and acuteness generally lacking in that modest Englishman. As Paul to Jesus, and James Mill to Bentham, and Lenin to Marx, he was carrying a doctrine to lengths which would have made it unrecognisable to the Master.

Condillac tried everything to explain the genius of that marvellous statue of his. First of all he tried the development of language, then its development of the faculty of 'attending' to what was most useful to it, then the sovereignty among the senses of the tactile sense. The trouble was that Condillac's 'mind' never seemed to have a bottom to it. His was a psychology of the top storey only. For there to be experience there must be an experient, or something that experiences. The statue had to be conscious of itself (its self) before it could be conscious of anything else. Locke, less happy, but more truly philosophical if only because he was more aware of the difficulties, more prepared to admit them, and therefore to 'rest content with half‹knowledge' like most Englishmen; Locke remains – and will always remain – a philosopher. Condillac must be content to remain a *Philosophe*. It was only after his total environmentalism that the furthest development of the *Philosophes'* position, as it is seen in the work of Helvétius, was possible.

In 1758 Condillac became tutor to the Prince of Parma (a nephew of Louis XV) and was absent from France for nearly ten years. It was in this connection that he drew up his *Cours d'études*, a work in sixteen volumes, amounting to a giant conspectus of modern pedagogy. '*Une masse imposante*, it has been called. But as someone said, 'Doubtless this scarcely gives us an exact notion of the lessons he gave to the Prince.' Perhaps it is the nearest Condillac came to constructing his own

Encyclopedia, or at least its principles. The departments of the work are devoted to Mind, Education, Logic, Mathematics, Economics and Animals. The education of youth should proceed like the education of the human race. The earliest state would be education in and by the immediate environment and its necessities, then the education of taste, and finally education in the most advanced form of human activity – speculation. He summed it up in the words, 'The history of the human mind showed me . . . the order to follow in the instruction of the Prince.' And like Rousseau, he believed that 'a sound educational method must follow that of nature'. He would go so far as to define the teacher's task as 'to assist in the process of self-instruction'.

He might have proceeded to undertake the education of the sons of the Dauphin, which would have afforded us an excellent example of the *Philosophe* replacing the Jesuit in key positions governing the future. He declined the task, however. His employment at Parma had secured him a substantial pension. He now retired to spend his last years with his niece in the country, near Beaugency, living the simple life and caring for the poor, perhaps making up for his former years by setting an example of religious devotion. He also wrote on government, in its relation to trade, on logic, and on 'the language of calculus'. He died in 1780. 'The merit of Condillac is very great', James Mill was to write in the enthusiasm of a British 'opposite number' of the *Philosophes*. He prizes in especial his powers of brief and concise expression, so that, while lacking originality, 'he left the science of the human mind in a much better state than he found it'. To no one, with the exception of Locke, his master, was the progress of the human mind more largely indebted. Yet it is more than possible that Condillac's crystal clarity did little service to his chances of survival. He possessed few if any of the features which were to serve as preservative in the cases of other *Philosophes*: style, wit, imagination, colour, he had none of these. For example, much of the science of Diderot has long gone out of date, but it remains alive by reason of the man's warmth and vitality as a writer, while Condillac's admirable writings are left as high and dry on the shores of intellectual history as the works of Herbert Spencer. He fulfils precisely Professor Oakeshott's reproach to the *Philosophes* when he wrote: 'He does not know what it is to be perplexed.' There are no blurred edges to his work, no uncertainties, no sign of a contradiction. Nor are there any of those modest guesses which abound in Locke, and from which other thinkers were to gather seminal hints for the future. There were no 'growing-points' and his work is vulnerable because it was too complete, too simple.

And yet Condillac wrote a whole book to warn his fellows against the delusions of system‚makers. His *Traité des systèmes* (1749) is a master‚ piece. A great part of the book consists of a rigorous examination of Aquinas, Descartes, Leibniz, Malebranche, Spinoza and others as thinkers who have based vast intellectual systems on general abstract principles for which evidence is claimed *a priori*. He finds it possible to give temporary assent to systems based on conjecture which experience of particulars seems likely to validate eventually, Diderot being one of the authors of this class of system. But the only really fruitful system he finds to be derived purely from established facts: the sovereign example being the inductive system of Newton. Reading his book, one feels that he is continually framing statements, warnings, that should have been written in letters of fire above the *Philosophes'* doorways.

> Permit the Philosopher to attempt, from the depths of his study, to set matter in motion, and he will dispose of everything as he pleases; nothing will resist him.
>
> As for suppositions, the imagination makes them with so much pleasure and so easily. It is from such foundations that one creates and governs the universe. All this costs no more than a dream, and philosophers dream easily.
>
> When one adds curiosity to a little imagination, one immediately begins to look into the distance, one wants to include everything and know everything. One ignores details, the things under one's eyes; one takes flight into unknown lands, and one constructs systems.

On bâtit des systèmes . . . an echo of Voltaire's gibe in *Micromégas*. The Ship of Fools, or the boat full of *Philosophes*, when alarmed and mystified, is overcome with panic. The purser says his prayers and recites exor‚ cisms, the sailors fall to swearing, 'and the *Philosophes* on board fell to system‚making' as if it were a game, a kind of intellectual version of patience.

It is sad that Condillac should only be remembered as the *Philosophe* who ruined Locke, for in the process he made the Lockeian psychology the orthodoxy of the liberal thinkers of the eighteenth century. The total environmentalism which he drew from Locke made possible the work of Helvétius and (by direct descent from Helvétius) that of Ben‚ tham and the English Utilitarians. In Helvétius's *De l'esprit* (1758) it emerged openly in the catchword (or war‚cry) *'L'éducation peut tout'*. It is hardly surprising that Bentham's greatest disciple, James Mill, should have said: 'No man has done as much towards perfecting the theory of education as Mons. Helvétius.' Condillac really was eclipsed with the eclipse of the concept of the 'instrumental mind', or the notion of the mind as a machine into which ideas are fed via the senses. Western man has ceased to talk about the mind in terms of machines, or box-cameras, or dark closets with chinks in them, or with tops and bottoms. The change has come with the abandonment of mechanistic or concrete language in the discussion of the mental world. It is part of the process by which men have detected the 'category-mistake', or what Whitehead calls 'misplaced concreteness', arising from the world of clockwork models and mechanical toys, the world of Descartes. Such language is now reserved for discussion of the physical structure of the brain, while the mind is now conceived as consisting wholly of thoughts, not as 'containing' them. There is not, and there never was, a *tabula rasa*, a clean sheet or a wax surface waiting to be written on. Even the age of the gramophone record has failed to revive this way of thinking of the mind. The mind does not precede thought. It is thought.

It is just as well that Condillac won fame for a fundamental fallacy, for the Utilitarians were able to frame their valuable programmes of reform on it. Without Condillac there would have been no Helvétius, and thereby no Bentham.

PART II
The Second Generation

Chapter Six

THE MAN OF LANGRES

LIKE a species perfecting itself in the evolutionary course of nature, the type of the *Philosophe* reached perfection in Diderot. He is one of the great archetypes, springing to mind at the mention of the name of philosopher or poet, like Immanuel Kant staring at the egg in his hand while boiling his watch,[1] or like Shelley sloping along with flashing eyes and floating hair. There is in each an element of caricature. Shelley is a little too much of the poet; Kant exhibits more than enough of the characteristics of the philosopher. Diderot scribbling in his garret, laughing and weeping in turns, and talking all the time, is the *Philosophe in excelsis*. Talking above all else. 'A great man,' said Voltaire after meeting him, 'but nature has refused him an essential talent: that of dialogue' – a strange comment on the author of *L'Entretien entre d'Alembert et Diderot, L'Entretien d'un père avec ses enfants,* and *L'Entretien d'un philosophe avec la maréchale.* Even had it been true, he more than made up for it by his prolific writings. While the Acts of the Christian Apostles, Carlyle said, can be read in an hour, 'the Acts of the French Philosophes . . . lie recorded in whole acres of typography and would furnish reading for a lifetime'. Diderot's acts alone make up twenty volumes in Assezat and Tourneaux's edition of the *Œuvres complètes,* and that still leaves the hundreds of articles he wrote for the Encyclopedia, 200 on religion alone. Some of his greatest works, like *Le Neveu de Rameau,* were not published until after his death. And now there are the *Salons.*

The first ten years of his life after leaving home for Paris were a period of Bohemian garret-life, years of hand-to-mouth existence. He had been to the Jesuit school at Langres and had begun training for the priesthood until his father caught him in the act of running away to Paris and then proceeded to take him there, where he studied at the Collège d'Harcourt and at St-Louis-le-Grand. The solicitude of his father in these early unsettled years may help to account for the fact that the youth developed

[1] Some have said that the original hero of this anecdote was the poet Cowper.

a happy, ebullient, sanguine temperament, well-adapted to the sociable life of the *Philosophe* as he always portrayed it. If a father ever inadver-tently made a *Philosophe* of his son it was the good Didier Diderot, master-cutler of Langres in Champagne. If a man's home town has much to do with it, Langres with its many weather-vanes may be accredited with having set a veering head on his shoulders. He said himself: 'The man of Langres has a head on his shoulders like a weather-cock on the top of the church-spire.' He was always subject to sudden changes, swinging impulsively in every direction as he cried the state of the intellectual atmosphere. Ernst Cassirer said of him, that he was of all the thinkers of his century the one who 'possessed the keenest sense for all the intellectual movements and transitions of that epoch'. He is only to be understood in terms of 'an instinctive fluidity of mind'. His intellec-tual and moral life was a kind of dance, or a fencing-match. 'For him the exercise of thought is not a game of patience, but an adventure.' Like Thomas Hardy he found that life was not so much a scientific game as an emotion. This is what the professional philosophers have always found it so hard to forgive him. At every turn Diderot brings to mind the jocund temperament of the artist. It is useless to charge him with inconsistency or with not staying with a 'system'. His advice was 'have a system, I agree, but don't let yourself be ruled by it'. Like the weather-vane, he was constantly 'returning upon himself'. As he once said to d'Alembert: 'If you come to think of it, my friend, you will find that our truest opinions are not those from which we have never strayed but those to which we most often return.' He was of a new generation, that of Condillac, Rousseau and David Hume. When Diderot was born, Voltaire was twenty, Montesquieu twenty-five, Fontenelle fifty-six. Their writings were the 'classics' of his youth. He could not remember Louis XIV. To him, 'philosophy was not born of a reflection, but of a con-tinuous experience'. That was how his life went in the Latin Quarter, not 'an ordering of values', or a revelation, but rather 'the reflection of life in a keen, enthusiastic and eminently open intelligence'. The Quar-tier de Saint-Médard where Diderot lodged hummed with the rich and vigorous life of Grub Street combined with the fanatical rowdiness of a Welsh revivalist meeting. It was the scene of the *convulsionnaires*, hordes of Jansenist fanatics (a breed of 'Catholic Puritans'), who went into trans-ports and inflicted torments upon themselves in the hope of inducing the descent of divine grace. Amidst revolting scenes of mass hysteria they sought the working of miracles at the tomb of the Jansenist deacon, Pâris. The young man from Langres kept himself alive by writing other people's sermons, teaching mathematics to other people's children, translating English books, reading, always reading, and watching the pullulating life of the poor of a great capital. After the formal learn, ing of St,Louis,le,Grand and the Collège d'Harcourt it was second education. His classics were Bayle and Fontenelle and Voltaire. The greatest influence came from England via *Lettres philosophiques, ou sur les Anglais*, and the writings of the English deists, Pope, Boling, broke, Clarke and Shaftesbury; most of all Shaftesbury, whose *Prin, ciples of Moral Philosophy* he translated for a bookseller, making notes as he went along. After the dry, steely, short,winded style of Voltaire he found Shaftesbury warm, eloquent, emotionally alive. It was Shaftesbury who revealed him to himself, indeed who made him a *Philosophe*.

At this time of day it is perhaps strange to imagine anyone being inspired by that polite deist, the prim and shallow grandson of Dryden's great Achitophel, although he has been latterly recognised by literary historians as an important source of the Romantic sensibility in his century. To translate Shaftesbury into French in 1745 was a veritable eye,opener, not as regards a body of ideas, perhaps, but as a tempera, ment. Diderot found in him his affinity. He had carefully studied *Characteristics* (1711) and the *Letter on Enthusiasm* (1708). Principally he was enchanted by the Englishman's youthful fervour, his emphasis on the interdependence of happiness and virtue, and especially on the converse of this, the barren nature of asceticism. To be virtuous, Shaftesbury told him, it was necessary to be happy. The sources of morality, of social sense and even of poetic creativity, he now learnt, were not to be found in abnegation or asceticism but in one's personal *chaleur*. Our happiness is bound up with that of others, in social virtue, charity, beneficence, generosity, the social virtues.

> The generous Ashley, friend of man,
> Who scanned his nature with a brother's eye . . .

as James Thomson called him, was saying at some length what Alex, ander Pope said briefly in his *Essay on Man*, that God and Nature had so 'fixed the general frame' as to bid 'self,love and social be the same'. Commonplace enough in the land of Locke with its commercial morality, but a revelation in the Quarter of the *convulsionnaires*. Shaftesbury's rejection of the divinity of Christ, of miracles, of the divinely,inspired Scriptures and the infallible Church, his easy dismissal of both anthropo, morphism and fanaticism, his defence of deism against both superstition and atheism: all alike took hold of Diderot in an outright conversion. It is, of course, true that the process was assisted by the preparatory influence of Voltaire and Bayle and by the secret pioneering of half a century of anti/Christian propaganda by clandestine literature.

On the strength of all this Diderot wrote his first book, *Pensées philosophiques*, in 1746. The story that he composed it between Good Friday and Easter Sunday probably refers to its assembly from his long labour at note/taking while engaged on his translation of Shaftesbury,[1] but it sets the pace, and the tone, of his long career as a writer. It also was premonitory by the fact that it was at once condemned by the Paris Parlement to be burnt by the common hangman.[2] Nevertheless it went into fifteen editions in his lifetime and has never ceased to be read, the last critical edition appearing in 1950.

He opens his book with a defence of the passions, striking at once a note which has too often been thought dumb in the keyboard of the age of reason: 'Nevertheless it is only the passions and the great passions which can raise the soul to great things.' It is like listening to one of the great Romantics of the latter end of the century.[3] 'Without passion there can be nothing sublime in either our ways or our works; the fine arts will return to childishness, and virtue will be mere trifling.' Mediocre passions make men commonplace. Frustrated passions degrade extra/ ordinary men. 'Constraint destroys the greatness and the energy of nature.' Not mortification but harmonisation of the passions should be our object. Beating the breast and tearing the flesh in order to appease a living God is the madness of fanaticism. The savage indictment of the *convulsionnaires* of Saint/Médard which constitutes the seventh of the *Pensées philosophiques* must be got out of the way before Diderot can come to his real business, which is the defence of deism against both atheism and superstition.

The defence, at first sight, seems to be based on the usual contem/ porary (frequently Voltairian) lines of attack on the foundations of Christian revelation. Atheism is denounced as a disease of the mind; fanaticism as a form of ill/health of sensibility. There is as much blas/ phemy in making God a God of fear[4] as there is in denying his existence.

---

[1] His translation of the *Inquiry concerning Virtue or Merit* was published in 1745.

[2] Laurent Durand gave Diderot fifty louis for it, but his name was not given on the title/page, so that he escaped prosecution while enjoying the publicity.

[3] e.g. Coleridge on deep thinking and deep feeling.

[4] 'There are some people of whom it is better to say not that they fear God but that they are afraid of Him.'

There is a good deal of conventional championship of reason against faith here; but what is worth particular notice, as especially typical of Diderot, is his constant social concern. He advocates emancipation from Christian revelation not simply in the interests of a Christian *sagesse*, but in the interests of 'social hygiene'. Like Shaftesbury reacting against the Calvinist excesses in the London of Queen Anne, Diderot upholds '*l'intérêt social de déisme*' against the Parisian excesses of Jansenist mobs. Both extremes, atheism and fanaticism, are best defeated by natural religion. It is likewise important to grasp the sincerity of Diderot's deism at this stage, since he was soon to move on to materialism, and it is all too easy to see his deism at the earlier period as a mere cloak for a fundamental scepticism. Even more important is his recourse to natural scientists rather than to the metaphysicians as allies against atheism. Not only does he embrace the classical deism of Newton based on mathematicophysical science which would strive to defeat atheism by satisfactory proofs for the existence of a sovereign intelligence, a 'supreme artificer', clockmaker and clockwinder, presiding over the great machine of nature with its wheels and pulleys, springs and weights. He goes further: to the scientists of *living* nature, the anatomists and naturalists. 'The sublime meditations of Malebranche and Descartes', the subtleties of ontologists like Anselm and Spinoza, are far less effective in shaking the atheists than 'a single observation of Malpighi'. It is not from the metaphysicians or even the mathematicophysicists, that atheism is receiving its most vital attack, but from the biological sciences making headway with Réaumur, Buffon, microbiologists like Bonnet, Redi, Malpighi, Abraham Trembley and the Abbé Needham, all of whose names begin to crop up in Diderot's work at this time. These are the men of science, sometimes dabblers, who attend not the planets but the microbes, the men who began to come into their own with Charles Raven's *Life of John Ray* after the giant form of Newton had blocked out the light for so long.

Why did Diderot turn from Newtonian physics to the science of microbiology, from the telescope to the microscope? Because he realised that any mathematicophysical proof of deity was vulnerable to the atheist's attack. It was well enough to argue that the wonderful clock of the universe postulated a clockmaker, but there was always the possibility that the whole wondrous system had come into existence by chance, by 'the fortuitous play of atoms'. In an age of gambling mania the argument generally took the form of a game of dice with moveable types. One throw out of many millions might result in the types coming to rest in an order composing the text of (say) the *Iliad*. Today a more popular image might be a monkey hitting a typewriter, and once in a million million times happening to knock out (say) the complete works of Shakespeare. As long as such contingencies may arise, however great the odds against, Diderot was prepared to admit that the atheist might have the better of the argument (or as he put it, *'cette comparaison lui donnerait beau jeu'*). It was to deal with this fatal weakness that he brought biology to the aid of physics. As long as the universe is just a clock the atheist might win. Once it is shown that the universe is not just a clock, the argument for its emergence from a chance combination of atoms in motion is inadequate. Biology provides proof not merely of design but of purpose. Hence Diderot rejoices in the marvellous mechanism of the lowest forms of organic life. The wing of a butterfly presents signs a thousandfold more indicative of the existence of God than does even our own power of thinking. Have you ever observed, he asks, in any man more intelligence, order, wisdom and reasonableness than in the mechanism of an insect? Is not Deity as clearly apparent in the eye of a fleshworm as in the works of the great Newton?[1] What an assertion! Yet it is an assertion that he is prepared to make. 'Unless I am greatly deceived this proof is worth a great deal more than those which are still laid down in the Schools.'

Already Diderot had gone far beyond Shaftesbury. He was interested in far more, and he belonged to a society which, by its very defects, encouraged intellectual adventure. There was no stopping in France, as there was in England.[2] Everything in the defective and unhappy state of politics and religion, let alone political economy, drove men on to the extremes of enquiry, to the utmost reaches of philosophy, to the bounds of critical analysis. Diderot could find in Shaftesbury *la chaleur*, the social concern of the *Philosophe*, but he leaves the somewhat smug and simpering[3] English milord far behind as he advances into the realm of biological science and in the direction of an early form of creative evolution. Within another seven years he is to write another sort of *Pensées*, not merely denominated *philosophiques* but specifically directed to the interpretation of nature, by which he intends its *interrogation*. This book never attracted the interest of the first, yet it is in many ways

---

[1] More familiar to us may be the argument about the case of the stag⁄beetle, and how a space exactly the length of the horn is left to accommodate it at the chrysalis stage.

[2] England's power to stop was admirably shown in the English⁄type Revolution of 1688.

[3] The adjective is George Saintsbury's.

an advance on it. Some have called it Diderot's *Discourse on Method*. In *Pensées sur l'interprétation de la nature* he sets in apposition, after a manner typical of the man of Langres, the diverse methods of Newton and Descartes, without offering a hint of their resolution. 'If it raises difficulties for you, I advise you to go and ask a Newtonian,' are his last words; 'for I tell you I don't know how to solve them.' He had begun the work with a disclaimer of dogmatic instruction. 'I am not proposing to instruct, but to exercise, your mind, and it matters to me very little whether you accept or reject my ideas, so long as they engage your whole attention.'

The weather-vane is on the swing once more, veering towards the quarter from whence the newest intellectual change is to come. The great age of mathematical science is passing: within a century there will not be three great geometers in Europe. The career of this great science is to be cut short. It will be left where men like the brothers Bernouilli, Euler, Maupertuis, d'Alembert left it; they having sighted the Pillars of Hercules, men will go no further. The future rests with the sciences of living nature, and the last twenty-six *Pensées* consist of examples and *conjectures*, touching the origins of matter, the generation of life, organic molecules, electricity and the transformation of species. The names cited are not Newton and Descartes but those of medical men like Boerhaave and Haller, naturalists like Buffon and Linnaeus. There is even a con-jecture which foreshadows the subject of *L'Entretien entre d'Alembert et Diderot*, the daring work which, though written in 1769, remained unprinted for nearly half a century after Diderot's death: whether there is any fundamental difference between *la matière morte* and *la matière vivante*? Knowing what we now know about fermentation, the action of microscopic insects in 'dead' matter, the existence of microbes, can we really say that 'living molecules can only recover life, after having lost it, in order to lose it again, and so on for ever and ever'? It is at this point that the *Philosophes* arrived at their own peculiar version of everlasting life.

Diderot's welcome to the advent of the sciences of living nature, his dissatisfaction with mathematics and the 'abstract' as tools for the interro-gation of nature, was not simply the result of contemporary progress in the organic sciences, for in point of fact they were behind hand, as Diderot himself complains. One result of their comparatively backward state was that many of the ideas built upon them by Diderot were built on sand – for example the notion of spontaneous generation of life, a notion attractive to men busy in trying to get rid of the idea of Creation.

After all, Diderot and his confrères were *hommes engagés*. There was little that was objective about their science, or about most other things, and they would jump at any theory promising to enable them to dispense with theology. To establish the sciences of life on their own independent basis was their own form of *écrasez l'infâme*. To vindicate science as supreme in its own realm – the realm of nature – was to repudiate what were called 'the physics of Moses', to repel theological intrusion in fields where it was both inappropriate and obstructive. To do this in the interest of increasing man's control over his world was a large part of the liberal intention. Deism was of little use for this purpose. Diderot belonged to a later generation than Voltaire and deistic conservatism, one or two generations later than Fontenelle and his polemical scepticism. Fontenelle was a mathematician, at least a mathematical propagandist. Diderot's preference for biological science was in part at least the off-spring of his passion for the little creatures of natural history, the fascination of germs, microbes, the butterfly, the polyp, the tree-louse, all of which belong to his pantheon. The stellar universe with its enormous dimensions seems to belong naturally to the mathematician, but to the poet, the novelist, the craftsman there is endless delight in the sight of God in a grain of sand or a flower.

The eclipse of mathematics and physics by zoology, botany and ento-mology at this time, the climatic change which Diderot represents in his dealings with science, arose from the fact that mathematics has for its object (indeed, its subject-matter) certain abstractions that do not corre-spond exactly with anything in the material realm. It fails to grapple with the concrete reality of the actual world. In order to interrogate nature it was necessary to replace the counting, calculating method of the mathematics of the seventeenth century with a direct attack upon the profusion of reality, regardless of whether it could be described in clear and precise concepts, or reduced to measurement and number. This approach to nature – the concern with the substantive – even the sub-stantial – reality of the world of phenomena, had its ideological value too. Substantive nature, her health, her normality, was a criterion and con-sorted well with the popular interest in a way that isosceles triangles and the differential calculus did not. By the 1740s 'Nature', and 'Natural History' had become the popular passion of the age. 'Nature unveiled' was the latest image of man's progress. It was about to take place, after centuries of concealment. There was something dramatic about it. As Montesquieu wrote: 'One would say that Nature acted like those virgins who long preserve their most precious possession, and then allow them-

Fontenelle, 1657–1757

The doyen of the *Philosophes*, who lived to within a few days of his hundredth year, which has been said to be a tribute to the health-giving qualities of 'philosophy'.

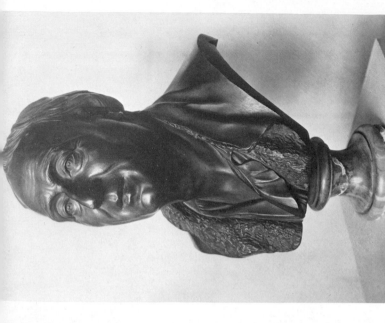

d'Alembert, 1717–83, and Diderot, 1713–84

Diderot was the father of the Encyclopedia and d'Alembert was for some time his partner as Editor. D'Alembert wrote the preliminary discourse for the work.

A salon in session

Condillac, 1715–80

Younger son of le vicomte de Mably, he devoted his life to developing John Locke's theories of the human understanding.

Helvétius en famille, *1715–71*

Author of *De l'esprit* (1758), considered to be a revolutionary work. Madame Helvétius was one of the most beautiful women of the age. Their younger daughter, Élisabeth, opened the ball with the aged Fontenelle (see p. 3).

La Mettrie, 1709–51, author of Man, a Machine, *1750*

Sometimes called the buffoon among the *Philosophes,* and certainly the most outrageous of them. It was, quite simply, a scandal to honour La Mettrie with the name of '*Philosophe*', d'Alembert said.

Malesherbes, 1721–94

As *Directeur de la Libraire,* 1750–63, he supervised the publishing trade when the Encyclopedia was coming out, and was able to protect it from the danger of sup⁄ pression in 1759. The Encyclopedists were wrong not to believe in Providence, it was said, since Providence gave the censorship to M. de Malesherbes.

Marquis de Condorcet, 1743–94

The Marquis was a distinguished mathematician who turned his science to political purposes. A disciple of Turgot, he went into hiding when the Girondins gave way to the Jacobins in 1793, and died in captivity in the following year. Condorcet was in all respects the noblest of the *Philosophes*, leaving to the world his 'Sketch for a historical picture of the progress of the human mind', which he wrote on the steps of the guillotine.

selves to be ravished in a moment of what they have preserved with such care and defended with such constancy.' The frontispiece of the 1751 edition of the Encyclopedia was to show the goddess Nature cling-ing to her veil while Truth, Reason and Philosophy seek to draw it away.

Chapter Seven

VINCENNES

In 1746 Diderot undertook the translation of Dr Robert James's *Diction-ary of Medicine* for the firm of Briasson, David and Durand. It was out of this work that arose the mighty project of the Encyclopedia and his management of it. In the previous year he had assisted, in an advisory capacity, in the translation of Chambers's *Encyclopedia, or Universal Dictionary of the Arts and Sciences*, a work first published in two volumes in 1728. It was Briasson who proposed Diderot for the task, and another associated publisher, Le Breton, agreed to offer him the editorship at a hundred livres a month. The official appointment is dated 16 October 1747, with Jean le Rond d'Alembert as his assistant with the special charge of mathematics. Diderot transformed the operation from the modest one of translation to the gigantic project of a synthesis of the French genius, or 'the monument of our country'. The French genius was great enough, he held, to write its own Encyclopedia without limiting itself to a transcription of Ephraim Chambers.

He had scarcely embarked on the production of the first volume when he was arrested and sent to the fortress of Vincennes. This was in July 1749. He was released in November. The publishers, and Diderot him-self, had represented to Comte d'Argenson, Minister of War, that it was impossible for them to spare the indispensable man for so valuable a project as the Encyclopedia, a work dedicated to the glory of France and the shame of England, recently beaten at Fontenoy in the War of the Austrian Succession. France at the height of the *ancien régime* was a proud and highly civilised country. Only two years later the censorship was to be entrusted to Lamoignon de Malesherbes, a young nobleman whose sympathies were all on the side of the new ideas,[1] and it was largely by his connivance that the Encyclopedia was carried to a triumphant conclusion over the next fifteen years. Diderot's incarceration during the summer months of 1749, however, was not on account of his work for the

[1] In the Revolution he was to perish on the guillotine for having tried to save Louis XVI.

Encyclopedia, which had as yet produced no fruit, but for his authorship of a certain *Lettre sur les aveugles à l'usage de ceux qui voient*. This at least was the official story, although it would seem that his arrest was simply one item in a general clear-up in 1749 of disturbers of the tranquillity of the public mind at a time of set-backs in India and North America, and defeats at sea. On the whole things were not going well for France, and at such times it was generally adjudged well to make a few sacrifices to the gods of orthodoxy. Diderot was known as a dangerous young man, and into prison he went along with 'a flock of abbés, scientists and *littérateurs*', not to mention certain professors of the university and reverend doctors of the Sorbonne, etc. Evidently Diderot was in good company. When police inspector Berryer questioned him a whole succession of works was mentioned, all but one of which he denied, and that one he said he burned.

While the general situation would probably have fetched Diderot into prison in July 1749, it was a personal quarrel that made it certain. He had managed to offend people in high places, notably Madame Dupré de St-Maur, who was a friend of the Minister of War, Comte d'Argenson. The occasion was a certain surgical operation conducted by René Antoine Ferchault de Réaumur (biologist, entomologist, inventor, metallurgist, naturalist, physician), whose protégé, a certain Prussian oculist, was operating for cataract.[1] Diderot secured an invitation to be present, an opportunity eagerly awaited by the philosopher-scientists of the age, for what happened when the bandages were removed from the patient's eyes would be crucial to the 'sensational philosophy', in particular the question whether the patient, able to see for the first time in his life, would be able to distinguish by sight between objects whose difference in shape he had previously detected only by touch. Philosophers like Locke and Berkeley had mostly thought the answer would be no, but the chance for philosophy to be tested by surgery was too priceless to be missed. Diderot was greatly chagrined by the outcome. When the bandages were lifted it was obvious that the patient had experienced sight before, and Diderot said so. The suspicion was that Réaumur had already given a private exhibition to his friend, Madame Dupré de St-Maur, or (in Diderot's words, as generally reported) 'that he preferred the eyes of a senseless pretty woman to those of persons capable of serious judgement'. It was a stupid fracas. For one thing, Madame Dupré was a lady who prided herself on her anatomical knowledge, and the fact that her eyes had been called pretty did not mollify

---

[1] Known as 'Cheselden's operation' from the English surgeon who successfully demonstrated it in 1728.

her. She took the tale to d'Argenson, who admired her, and Diderot was promptly rounded up with the rest of the suspects of that season. He was not, however, deterred from making some researches of his own. He went to see and interrogate another patient, known as 'the blind wine-grower of Puiseaux', and he looked into the case of Nicholas Saunderson, the blind Professor of Mathematics at Cambridge (1682–1739).

The blind wine-grower told him that he thought of sight as a kind of touch, the eyes being 'an organ on which the air produces the same effect as my stick upon my hand'. Diderot also learnt that the blind usually lack humane feelings since they have never experienced the visible signs of suffering. Nor do they set much value upon modesty, and but for the cold they would probably have little notion of the use of clothing. 'Ah, Madame,' Diderot exclaims to his mistress, to whom he addressed the *Lettre sur les aveugles*, 'how different is the morality of a blind man from ours . . . and, if a being should have a sense more than we have, how woefully imperfect would he find our morality!' Like Fontenelle with his *habitants* and Voltaire with his visitors from other planets in *Micro-mégas*, Diderot was hard on the track of the relativity of morals. The whole point of his work on *les aveugles*, and the head and front of his offence, was to establish the relative nature of our ideas of ethics and religion. A physical abnormality involves a total transformation of spiritual outlook.

As for Professor Saunderson, he was disappointing if one stuck to the Memoir prefixed to his *Algebra*, but Diderot did not stick to it. He was not to be baulked by lack of evidence. He proceeded to invent a death-bed speech for the Professor in which he said everything that Diderot would have wished. He pretended to derive this 'evidence' from a book attributed to one of Saunderson's disciples. He even went so far as to invent a name, 'William Inchlif', for the disciple. Nicholas Saunderson was a Fellow of the Royal Society of London, and the Society took Diderot's conduct very much amiss, and indeed his reputation for 'sound scholarship' was never to recover. The scholarly world probably thought his incarceration at Vincennes a very mild punishment for his audacity.

The death-bed observations attributed to Professor Saunderson were designed to refute deism, and the *Lettre sur les aveugles* is premonitory to Diderot's final position as a materialist. The dying mathematician is made to reject 'the magnificent spectacle of nature' as evidence of design. 'I have been condemned to pass my life in darkness', he protests; 'and yet you cite wonders which I cannot understand, and which are only evidence for those who can see as you do. If you want to make me believe in God you must make me touch him.' And why should he regard as miraculous the wonderful mechanism of his own organs? Why must we always treat everything beyond our own powers as the miraculous handi‚ work of God? We need a little less pride and a little more philosophy. To call in a Supreme Being in order to cut a difficult knot is only to create another knot more difficult than the first. And what becomes of 'the admirable order of nature' when one conjectures that the world was brought into being out of matter in a state of fermentation? Saunderson conjectures that 'in the beginning when matter in a state of ferment brought this world into being, creatures like myself were of very common occurrence'. Probably the history of nature is the history of countless false starts and failed experiments? 'How many faulty or incomplete worlds have been dispersed and perhaps formed again, and are dispersed at every instant in distant regions of space which I cannot touch nor you behold, but where motion continues, and will continue, to combine masses of matter, until they have found some arrangement in which they may finally persevere?' What is the 'marvellous order of nature', what are its 'wonderful adaptations', except metaphysical entities existing in your own mind?

At Vincennes Diderot assumes the final form of the *Philosophe*. Nothing concentrates a man's mind more than the knowledge that he is to be hanged in a fortnight, Dr Johnson thought, and, although Diderot was in no danger of hanging, he at once found himself stripped of his creature‚comforts and – what was no less essential to a man of his habits – the ordinary facilities for writing and reading. For a short time he was thrown back upon bare essentials: he who was to spend the rest of his life at large in a literary emporium was reduced to one or two books he carried with him, and his own ingenious imagination. As editor of the Encyclopedia he was to have everything in his hands that was worth reading, but for some twenty‚eight days in the stifling summer of 1749, he was locked up in a dim dungeon with a copy of *Paradise Lost*, a pocket Plato and something by Francis Bacon. Of course, the craftsman's son could be depended on to use his ingenuity. A toothpick served him as a pen. Powdered slate from the roof outside his window, steeped in wine, served as ink; nor, like a good *Philosophe*, did he neglect to give his fellows the benefit of his discoveries by inscribing the recipe on the wall of his cell for the use of later occupants. For writing‚paper he used the margins and blank pages of his copy of Milton's poem. Soon, when he was allowed other works, including Buffon's *Histoire naturelle*, he treated them in the same way. M. de Châtelet, the Warden of Vincennes, relaxed the discipline shortly, and he had boiled beef, tripe, and liver and onions, a bottle of wine a day, vegetables and fruit on Fridays. He was also allowed to walk in the garden, to receive visitors, and to have his wife to live with him. In August he signed a promise that he would not leave the château, its grounds, or the garden, nor 'cross the bridges'. It is said, however, that he soon levanted off to spy on his mistress at Champigny. It is typical of the looking-glass world of the France of the *ancien régime* that he was allowed to have some boxes of papers brought in, and that his quarters at Vincennes became the central office of the Encyclopedia enterprise for several weeks.

Diderot's copy of *Paradise Lost* has not survived, but his manuscript translation of the Apology of Socrates has come to light in the Fonds Vandeul. As M. Seznec has shown in his book, *Diderot et l'antiquité*, he possessed a concept of Socrates which may fairly be called *Le Socrate imaginaire*. When he referred to himself, as he did increasingly, as 'the philosopher' it was this fond projection he intended to convey. He identified himself with Socrates even to the possession of a Xantippe in the long-suffering Madame Diderot, a lady who certainly deserves more sympathy than reprobation. Nor was Diderot prepared to suffer the Socratic martyrdom in anything but his romantic imaginings. His pusillanimous conduct when interrogated by Berryer, the lieutenant of police, at the time of his arrest, is a repellent combination of truculence, evasiveness and downright lying. This was after the first few days of solitary confinement. 'I am afraid that you are going to be here for a while, M. Diderot,' said Berryer, 'for a long while.' It was only by an abject confession of his guilt on 13 August that he gained relaxation of the original severity of his treatment. It was a week later that he signed the undertaking not to leave the château or its grounds, and thereupon was permitted to receive his friends, his wife and the boxes of papers. One way or another he cut no very brave and certainly no Socratic figure at Vincennes. One thing this experience did for him, apart from clarifying his notion of himself as a *Philosophe*, was to scare him mortally of imprisonment and to make him circumspect for the rest of his life. It was fortunate for the great enterprise before him. He was to carry it through a long and perilous course with a tactical *ordonnance* which owed nothing to the example of Socrates and a great deal to the examples of Fontenelle and Voltaire.

One of his first visitors was Jean-Jacques Rousseau, his confrère with Condillac of the Café Panier-Fleuri. Rousseau was compelled by shortage

of funds to trudge all the way out to Vincennes on a burning day in
August. 'I found him greatly affected by his imprisonment', he records
in his *Confessions*. 'The dungeon had made a terrible impression on him,
and although he was comfortable in the château and allowed to walk in
a park that was not even surrounded by walls, he needed the society of
his friends to avoid giving way to melancholy.' Temperamentally the
two men were much alike in that both were intensely emotional, given to
endless animated talk and to the prolific shedding of (jubilant) tears.
They differed chiefly in the fact that Diderot alone was a great lover of
society and its achievements. It was on one of his visits to Vincennes that
summer that Rousseau conceived his prize essay for the Academy of
Dijon on the progress of the arts and sciences and whether it had been
beneficial or detrimental to virtue. It was Rousseau's furious intention to
blame the corruption of man, indeed his 'fall', upon the corrupt influence
of civilisation, a thesis that was to obsess him all the rest of his life.
Diderot encouraged him in this paradox, and when Rousseau won the
prize he got it into his head that his friend imagined himself to have been
its only begetter. The fact that he encouraged Rousseau in his first book
against the progress of the human race (to adapt Voltaire's description of
his second one) may perhaps be explained by a retrospective remark of
Diderot on the subject: 'Rousseau *had* to disagree with everyone else.'
Anyway, he knew his friend well enough to realise that he needed some
such paradox if he was to do justice to his innate eloquence and originality. Diderot's other great friend who visited him at Vincennes was a
very different character, Jean le Rond d'Alembert, his co-editor. Jean-
Jacques Rousseau, as time went on, turned out not only to be no *Philosophe*
but to be their arch-enemy.

Bernard Shaw recalls how in the 1860s he heard a gentleman in a Dublin
bookshop enquire for 'the works of the celebrated Buffoon', and he
assures us that in those days every literate person knew Buffon's *Natural
History* as well as he knew Aesop's *Fables*. The first volumes of this work
were hot from the press in the year of Diderot's incarceration at Vincennes, and it was one of the first things he asked for when he was
permitted to send out for books. He read it with delight, for it was not
only a delightful work in itself but it confirmed the attitude towards
nature which had been taking charge of his mind over the years of his
growth. It was one of the most handsome works of an age of handsome
writing. Georges-Louis Leclerc, Comte de Buffon (1707–88), made natural history a branch of literature at a time when there was no alienation

between science and letters. 'Letters, the dear and worthy object of my most constant passion!' he exclaimed in addressing the French Academy in 1775. For him, as for Montesquieu, literature was a generic term 'which embraces all studies, and covers the whole field of human knowledge.... All the problems of literature are those of life, of nature and of man.' And the reverse proposition, it often seems, was equally true. Buffon was author of the famous aphorism: '*Le style c'est l'homme même.*' Certainly Buffon's style was the Comte de Buffon; the style of the man of whom it may be said that, as Machiavelli wrote *The Prince*, and as Joseph Haydn composed music, in Court dress, so did the Comte de Buffon write natural history. In his study at the tower of Montbaud near Dijon, on the terrace high above the trees, with a grand prospect of Burgundy stretched at his feet, the Comte sat at his desk for twelve or fourteen hours a day, 'in gentleman's attire, with sword, powder and ruffles'. It was even insinuated that the Comte liked to dress nature and his own style as elegantly as he dressed himself. Whatever the truth of this, Buffon wrote like nature's major-domo. He wrote like a *Philosophe* too; that is, in order to be read pleasurably. 'Mandarin' his style may be held today, after the manner of Bossuet and Fénelon, and Gustave Flaubert. The danger was, as Renan says, 'concern for his style involved certain sacrifices of thought'. But the Comte de Buffon 'didn't see this danger, or had no qualms about it'. He cultivated 'nobility, gravity, majesty', and he did so 'without fear or blemish'. Diderot, who wrote as he spoke, whose prose was often as hotly disordered as his way of life, reading *L'Histoire de la nature* at Vincennes experienced it as a revelation. For here was a philosopher who approached nature not as a problem in geometry or a subject for classification, but as 'a lightsome chaos on which the Spirit of God is moving'.

It hardly needs to be said that this was not the language of Buffon, still less that of Diderot. It was in fact the language of the poet Coleridge speaking from the heart of the Romantic Revival more than fifty years later. What rejoiced Diderot in Buffon is best expressed in Coleridge's apostrophe to 'the man of understanding', the classifier, the worshipper of categories:

> Man of understanding, canst thou command the stone to lie, canst thou bid the flower to bloom, where thou hast placed it in thy classification? Canst thou persuade the living or the animate to stand separate even as thou hast separated them? And do not far rather all things spread out before thee in glad confusion and heedless intermixture, even as a lightsome chaos on which the Spirit of God is

moving? Do not all press and swell under one attraction, and live together in promiscuous harmony, each joyous in its own kind, and in the immediate neighbourhood of myriad others that in the system of thy understanding are distant as the poles?

To Buffon, the profusion and flexibility of organic life resists the cate-gory-maker. In the introduction to his *Histoire naturelle* he repudiates the monistic ideal of natural science and its imposition on all branches of scientific research. The mathematical method, consisting of a series of purely analytical propositions connected by the bond of strict necessity, is alien to organic nature, where we are not concerned with concepts of our own making but with nature itself. To attempt to divide it into classes and species produces only a system of nomenclature, not a system of nature. Linnaeus succumbed to this cult of mere *arrangement* of nature. His *Philosophia Botanica* was a treatise on the boast: '*Deus creavit, Linnaeus disposuit.*' – 'God proposes [creates], Linnæus disposes.' Buffon demanded that we reverse this procedure, applying the principle of connection, not of analytical differentiation, studying living creatures in their kinship, evolution and transformation, not in their differences. He tends towards an outright nominalism, concerning himself not with species or genera but only with individuals. So-called 'biological types' are not fixed and unalterable. Animal traits can change completely with time.

This is where modern intellectual history begins, with the abandon-ment of scholastic logic, definition by *genus proximum* and *differentia specifica* – which had passed from the schoolmen to the scientists of the seventeenth century. Mechanism, or the study of how things work, is no longer to be the sole and sufficient explanation of being, and being is no longer the source and explanation of becoming. Instead, becoming is the explanation of being. Nature is to be regarded as a universe in movement, everything everlastingly turning into something else. What exists at any one moment is what Diderot calls '*un ordre momentané*'. The essence of the order is 'transformism', to which he had given expression in the imaginary words of Professor Saunderson: 'What is this world, Mr Holmes, but a complex, subject to cycles of change, all of which show a continual tendency to destruction; a rapid succession of beings that appear one by one, flourish and disappear; a merely transitory symmetry and a momentary appearance of order?' His 'conjecture' as to whether there is any fundamental difference between *la matière morte* and *la matière vivante* at the end of his *Pensées sur l'interprétation de la nature* had raised the subject as a question. His *L'Entretien entre d'Alembert et Diderot* and *Le Rêve de d'Alembert* were to constitute a fantasy upon it.

C 2

Chapter Eight

LE RÊVE DE D'ALEMBERT

The fact is, it is very difficult to think cogently in metaphysics or ethics without being an anatomist, a naturalist, a physiologist and a physician.

DIDEROT

W HEN d'Alembert visited Diderot at Vincennes the two friends fell into each other's arms. Jean le Rond was the younger by some four years, but he looked younger still with his wide eyes, his mobile lips and his boyish smile. Quentin de La Tour has recorded his charm in a famous pastel portrait. Like the longevity of Fontenelle and the loquacity of Diderot, d'Alembert's smiling face transmits to posterity invincible testimony to the vitality of the species *Philosophe*. The illegitimate child of an artillery-officer and an unwilling nun, he had been named after the church of Saint-Jean-Le-Rond in Paris upon whose steps the baby had been found in a small wooden box. The notorious Madame de Tencin appears to have taken no further interest in the child. Having made money out of the financial schemes of John Law, she proceeded with her amours. The artillery-officer, Louis-Camus Destouches, provided him with a meagre income, and he grew up in the house of a certain Madame Rousseau, a glazier's wife, who lived in the Rue Michel-le-Comte. 'You will never be anything but a philosopher,' she would say, 'and what is a philosopher? A madman who torments himself during his lifetime in order that people may speak of him when he is dead.' Jean le Rond assumed the name of d'Alembert and went to school at the Jansenist Collège des Quatre Nations where he failed to take any interest in theology but revealed a gift for mathematics. He took his bachelor's degree at eighteen and proceeded to the Académie des Sciences on the strength of his communications on the refraction of solid bodies and the mechanics of fluids. His *Traité de dynamique* and other works in the field of theoretical physics promoted his fame even beyond the frontiers of France in the 1740s and gave him a *cachet* in society as one of the leading mathematicians of his day. He still lived in his tiny room in Madame Rousseau's house, but he became an habitué of the *salon* of Madame Geoffrin, where his energy, his gaiety, and his pleasing gift of mimicry made him immensely popular. The source of his playfulness, Marmontel was to write, was a certain purity of soul, a freedom from the passions, the innocent enjoyment he took in his mathematical labours, 'the exclusive privilege of the exact sciences, which no other type of study can fully give'.

In many respects d'Alembert is the least publicised and yet the most likeable of the *Philosophes*. He is known to most people as an important mathematician and because his name appears with that of Diderot on the title-page of the Encyclopedia. Besides Quentin de la Tour's delicious pastel, which might have been drawn from any happy young man of the age, there is Thomas Carlyle's eulogy of the good man. 'A French author, d'Alembert (one of the few persons who deserve the honourable epithet of honest man), whom I was lately reading,' he told his mother in 1819, 'remarks that one who devoted his life to learning ought to carry for his motto, "Liberty, Truth, Poverty", for he that fears the latter can never have the former.' Carlyle was in the midst of his French studies, which gave us, among other things, his essay on Diderot, and no doubt he had come upon the story of d'Alembert's residence for many years in the poor glazier's house in the Rue Michel-le-Comte, long after he had become a distinguished figure in French society, and how he never lost his gratitude and kindness to his old foster-mother, indeed how he lived simply and frugally all his life. It was Diderot himself who said, on hearing of the death of his colleague: 'A great light has gone out.' Yet the elaboration of Diderot's final position as a materialist was to be carried through in writings which Julie de Lespinasse, d'Alembert's close friend, found offensive. In *Le Rêve de d'Alembert* and *L'Entretien entre d'Alembert et Diderot* the great mathematician attained a second, and dubious immortality.

Diderot composed these pieces in 1769 although they were not pub-lished until 1830. Lord Morley, writing his *Diderot* in 1878, called them 'as odious as anything since the freaks of filthy Diogenes in his tub'. However, while he thought them 'in form the most ugly and disgusting in the literature of philosophy', Morley was prepared to admit that they testified in their own way to their author's sincerity of interest in his subject. Nearly a hundred years later they found their way into the Penguin Classics, along with that undoubted masterpiece, *Le Neveu de Rameau*. It is not merely a matter of the arrival of what it is fashionable to call 'a permissive society'. It is rather that we are now in a position to see Diderot as a maker of the world in which men now live, and his writings as seminal to its mind and spirit. The fact that he had been responsible for such salacious works as *Les Bijoux indiscrets* in his younger days is no longer able to infect the attitude of readers to those works of his later years which caused offence to certain of his friends and con‑ temporaries. He himself said that there were some five or six pages in these dialogues that would make a woman's hair stand on end. He also knew that one must sometimes give to wisdom the air of madness in order to secure its admittance. Yet, along with a certain mathematical work, he said, these were the sole products of his pen with which he could feel wholly satisfied.

More than fifteen years had elapsed since *Les Pensées sur l'interpréta‑ tion de la nature* (1753) and twenty since the *Lettre sur les aveugles* (1749). The years between were the laborious years of the Encyclopedia. By 1765 the final volumes were published, and Hercules was released from his lab‑ ours. At last he was free to write what he liked instead of what he must, even if he was (as it turned out) not always free to publish it. He had another fifteen years to live, and before he died he was intent on completing the work which had been broken off when he went to Vincennes. The first of three pieces which make up *Le Rêve de d'Alembert* took up the question posed in Question 3 of *Pensée* 58: whether there is any funda‑ mental difference between *la matière morte* and *la matière vivante*. The dialogue begins with Diderot asking d'Alembert whether there is any fundamental difference between a man and a statue, between marble and flesh, and proceeding to argue that while a man possesses actual sensitivity a statue possesses latent sensitivity, and that a body can be made to pass from the latter state into the former. He goes on:

let me tell you the story of one of the greatest mathematicians in Europe. What was this wondrous being in the beginning? Nothing.

d'Alembert: Nothing! How do you mean? Nothing can come from nothing.

Diderot: You are taking words too literally. What I mean is that before his mother, the beautiful and scandalous Madame de Tencin had reached the age of puberty, and before the soldier La Touche had reached adolescence, the molecules which were to form the first rudi‑ ments of our mathematician were scattered about in the young and undeveloped organs of each. . . . Lo and behold, this rare seed takes form; it is carried, as is generally believed, along the Fallopian tubes and into the womb. It is attached thereto by a long pedicle, it grows in stages and advances to the state of foetus. The moment for its emer‑

gence from its dark prison has come: the new-born boy is abandoned
on the steps of Saint-Jean-le-Rond, which gave him his name. . . . How
did all this come about? Through eating and other purely mechanical
operations. . . . And anyone lecturing to the Academy on the stages in
the formation of a man or animal need refer only to material factors,
the successive stages of which would be an inert body, a sentient being
and then a being who can resolve the problem of the precession of the
equinoxes,[1] a sublime being, a miraculous being, one who ages, grows
infirm, dies, decomposes and returns to humus.

 d'Alembert: So you don't believe in pre-existent germs?

 Diderot: No. . . .

 d'Alembert: But without these pre-existent germs the original genesis
of animal life is inconceivable.

 Diderot: If you are bothered about the question of the priority of the
egg over the hen or of the hen over the egg, it is because you assume
that animals in the beginning were what they are at present. How
absurd!

Slightly later Diderot reverts to a favourite analogy, that of the 'bird-
organ', or *serinette*, one of those mechanical toys popular in the age of
Vaucanson. And what is the difference between the instrument called
'philosopher' and the instrument called 'clavichord'? We are, he will
say, 'instruments possessed of sensitivity. Our senses are so many keys
which are struck by things in nature around us, and often strike themselves.' At which, d'Alembert rejoins, 'if this sensitive and animated
clavichord were endowed with the further powers of feeding and re-
producing itself, it would be a living creature and engender from itself,
or with its female, little clavichords, alive and resonant'. Which is one of
those junctures at which we imagine d'Alembert smiling his enchanting
sourire de la philosophie, although Diderot, now in full spate, goes straight
on. 'No doubt,' he says, and proceeds to the lecturer's gesture of demon-
stration. 'Look at this egg: with it you can overthrow all the schools of
theology and all the churches in the world.' Which, after all, is what he
intends to do. Moreover, he is concerned to destroy his friend's 'sheer
metaphysico-theological balderdash', d'Alembert having stopped at
deism, which Diderot calls 'substituting for a cause which does exist
[Diderot's materialism] and which explains everything some other cause
which defies the understanding . . . which gives rise to innumerable
difficulties without solving any of them'. Good-naturedly enough,
d'Alembert simply asks: 'Well, suppose I give up this cause?' And
Diderot is able to conclude: 'That leaves only one substance in the uni-

---

[1] A problem on which d'Alembert had published his researches in 1749.

verse, in man, in animals. The bird-organ is made of wood, man is made of flesh. A canary is flesh, a musician is flesh differently organised . . .'

D'Alembert: Well, so long, my friend, good night and sleep well.
Diderot: Laugh if you like, but you will dream about this talk when your head is on your pillow.

The second piece, *Le Rêve* proper, begins with Julie de Lespinasse recording this very dream to Dr Bordeu, d'Alembert's doctor. The great mathematician has had, as Diderot predicted, a very disturbed night. 'What did he eat for supper?' asks the doctor. 'Nothing,' Mademoiselle de Lespinasse replies. 'I don't know where he spent the evening, but he came back with something on his mind.' *Le Rêve de d'Alembert* consists of Julie's account of d'Alembert's delirium and Dr Bordeu's commentary. It is a medical or physiological fantasy, Diderot's conjectural reflexions on his final position of transformistic materialism. It belongs to the category of literature which is best represented in the present century by a work like D. H. Lawrence's *Fantasia of the Unconscious*. Unlike Lawrence's piece of preachment, however, *Le Rêve* is put into the mouths of living characters, and while it sinks into what Morley called the filthy and everyone will call the disgusting, it also has the universal appeal of the best bawdy. After all, the author of *Le Rêve* was a friend and admirer of the writer of *Tristram Shandy* and was a not inconsiderable novelist. Certainly the real-life characters of *Le Rêve* are treated with the novelist's licence, subjected to the purposes of the fable with complete lack of the historian's scruple.

Little wonder that Julie de Lespinasse was horrified by what Diderot made her say, or that d'Alembert secured the suppression of the manuscript. Diderot scarcely knew the lady. All he wanted was a female recipient of the medical speculations of Dr Bordeu, somewhat as Fontenelle had invented the marquise for his pupil in delivering his astronomy lectures nearly a century earlier. The change of tone that had taken place since *Entretiens sur la pluralité des mondes* in 1686 is summed up by Diderot, the second-generation *Philosophe*, in a short passage of *Le Rêve* where Mademoiselle de Lespinasse cites Fontenelle's charming analogy of the rose and the gardener:[1]

Mlle de Lespinasse [referring to Dr Bordeu's remark about the transient being who believes in the immutability of things]: Like

[1] Towards the end of his final lecture (*le cinquième soir*) Fontenelle likens man's notion that the stars do not change to the notion that a rose might have that gardeners are immortal because in its short span of existence a rose has always seen the same gardener in the garden.

Fontenelle's rose, who declared that no gardener had ever been known to die?

Dr Bordeu: Exactly. That is both graceful and profound.

Mlle de Lespinasse: Why can't these philosophers of yours express themselves as gracefully as Fontenelle? We should understand them then.

Dr Bordeu: Frankly I am not sure that such a frivolous tone is suitable for serious subjects.

Mlle de Lespinasse: What do you call a serious subject?

Dr Bordeu: Well, universal sensitivity, the formation of a sentient being, its unity, the origin of animal life, its duration and all the questions these matters raise.

Mlle de Lespinasse: For my part I call all these things a lot of nonsense . . . and all of them absolutely useless . . .

But the doctor refuses to allow the lady to get away with such flippancy.

Dr Bordeu: Do you think, Mademoiselle, that it doesn't matter whether you accept or deny the existence of a Supreme Intelligence?

Mlle de Lespinasse: No.

Dr Bordeu: Do you think one can make up one's mind about a Supreme Intelligence without knowing exactly where one stands on the indestructibility of matter and its properties, the distinction between mind and matter, the nature of man and the reproduction of animal life?

Mlle de Lespinasse: No.

Dr Bordeu: Then these questions are not as pointless as you suggest.

Mlle de Lespinasse: But what has their importance to do with me if I can't possibly understand them?

Dr Bordeu: How can you if you don't go into them?

And go into them the doctor does, that is to say Diderot does. D'Alembert is made to dream, and to talk deliriously, first of all about the difference between continuity and contiguity in a swarm of bees, while Julie writes it all down and the doctor comments upon her notes. Indeed, because the doctor is really Diderot's mouthpiece, he not only understands but even anticipates what she reports to him. He is particularly interested in the difference between a single creature formed by continuous bees and a composite of many creatures contiguous to each other. The former is like men or fish, the latter like a polypous creature such as a worm or a serpent. The latter can multiply itself by division while the former cannot. Nevertheless, if a man could divide himself up into multitudes of microscopic men Julie imagines a whole society of different men, and the possibility of having a vast array of phials, each labelled, 'courtiers', 'prostitutes', 'kings', etc., etc. More interesting, however, is the fact that the dreaming d'Alembert is made to mutter: 'Voltaire can joke as much as he likes, but the Eelmonger is right' – a reference to Voltaire's gibe at John Turberville Needham[1] who had advanced the theory (in 1745) of the spontaneous generation of life by the formation of maggots ('eels' as Voltaire called the tiny wriggling creatures) in fermenting matter, thus obviating the need for outside agency – presumably divine creation. It was a favourite topic with materialists in the mid-eighteenth century, although it was disposed of by another abbé, Spallanzani, in 1767. It was a notion as old as Lucretius and might be thought to have been disposed of by Redi in the previous century. All that required to be done was to prove that the supposedly spontaneously generated creatures were not *de novo* but *ex ovo*, generated from eggs that had got into the container used in the experiment, entering through 'porous corks' and surviving by reason of insufficient boiling of the host-substance. Diderot was fond of playing with the idea of spontaneous generation, as he played with the idea of pathenogenesis as illustrated by the multiplication of the polyp ('Trembley's polyp'[2]) and the reproduction of the tree-louse, or the aphids,[3] by females alone, without male fertilisation (a nice example, it could be thought, of the 'virgin-birth').

Diderot had almost a schoolboy's passion for these details of contemporary science, and could rarely refrain from a reference to them, but d'Alembert's delirious remark here leads nowhere. It is immediately followed by what Lord Morley was doubtless referring to with his remark about the filthy tricks of Diogenes. For it is evident enough that at this point d'Alembert underwent an orgasm in his sleep, wishing to collect up the emitted sperm and send it to the Abbé Needham. 'Nothing must be lost if it might be useful. Mademoiselle, if that stuff could be collected into a phial and sent first thing in the morning to Needham . . .' It is not surprising perhaps that Mademoiselle's response is addressed to Bordeu: 'Doctor, don't you call this sheer raving?' To which the man of medicine replies tactfully: 'In your presence I suppose so.' After a long disquisition by the doctor on physical monstrosities, sleep, dreams, imagination, the secondary male characteristics of women and the feminine features

[1] John Turberville Needham (1713–81), an English Roman Catholic priest who lived in Italy and was known as 'the Abbé Needham'.

[2] Abraham Trembley (1700–84) in his *Mémoires pour servir à l'histoire d'un genre de polypes d'eau douce* (1744) discovered the self-generative habits of the fresh-water polyp: multiplication by fission.

[3] Charles Bonnet (1720–93), the distinguished entomologist, was the great pioneer of the study of the aphids.

of eunuchs and *castrati*, d'Alembert interrupts him with the mild reproof: 'I think you are talking smut to Mademoiselle de Lespinasse', to which Dr Bordeu rejoins: 'When you talk science you have to use technical terms.' He goes on doing so for another fifteen pages, after which he goes off to visit another patient, half-promising to return to dine with Mademoiselle de Lespinasse.

When he returns, d'Alembert has gone out, and the performance ends with a kind of epilogue in which Julie draws the doctor into a series of speculations on such topics as cross-breeding and the dangers of chastity. There is also a modern and common-sense defence of 'solitary vice', or auto-eroticism. The climax comes with Dr Bordeu's suggestions for the solution of that burning problem of eighteenth-century society: the servant problem, how to have enough of them, and how to keep them in their place. Allied to this is the problem of slavery in the colonies. Bordeu puts forward the project of breeding a race of footmen from goats:

> *Mlle de Lespinasse*: That's a fine idea. I already seem to see our duchesses' coaches followed by five or six great louts with goat-legs, and that delights me.
> *Bordeu*: But also we should no longer be degrading our fellow-men by forcing them to perform functions unworthy of them or of us.
> *Mlle de Lespinasse*: Better and better!
> *Bordeu:* And in our colonies we should stop bringing them down to the level of beasts of burden.
> *Mlle de Lespinasse*: Quick, quick, doctor, get to work and make us some goat-men.
> *Bordeu:* And you would allow that without any moral scruples?

His parting shot is his answer to her question: 'Where do these abomin-able tastes come from?'

> Always from some abnormality of the nervous system in young people, softening of the brain in the old, from the attraction of beauty in Athens, shortage of women in Rome, fear of the pox in Paris. Good-bye, good-bye.

Diderot was to write other things, and of scarcely less moral, or im-moral, daring. His novel, *Jacques le fataliste* (1773–4), inspired by *Tristram Shandy*, has been reconsidered by twentieth-century critics in the light of what has been achieved by Joyce and Proust and Virginia Woolf, though it is not a great novel. His *Supplément au voyage de Bougainville* (1771) was to outstrip Rousseau in its treatment of the theme of the Noble Savage. *Le Neveu de Rameau* (probably first drafted in 1761, finished in 1777 or 1779) is his masterpiece, though it was not in print until the nineteenth century, and has only recently appeared popularly in the Penguin Classics. The master of the Encyclopedia wrote his last works for the century of Joyce and Lawrence and Aldous Huxley. Indeed he had much affinity with the twentieth-century *Philosophe* who wrote *Back to Methusaleh*. Creative evolution held few secrets to the man who made Dr Bordeu say:

> He is right; the organs produce the needs, and conversely the needs produce the organs . . . The original shape of a creature degenerates or perfects itself through necessity and habitual functioning. We walk so little, work so little, but think so much that I wouldn't rule out that man might end by being nothing but a head.

Bernard Shaw, however, would never have allowed Mademoiselle Julie to protest: 'Nothing but a head! a head! that's not much use. For my part I was hoping that with unlimited love-making . . . What awful ideas you are putting into my head!'

Chapter Nine

MAN A MACHINE

It is, quite simply, an outrage to philosophy to call a La Mettrie a
Philosophe.   D'ALEMBERT

IN 1750 a book was published in London bearing the title:

MAN A MACHINE
wherein
The several systems of philosophers
in respect of the Soul are examin'd;
The different States of the Soul are shown to
be relative to those of the Body;
The Diversity between Man and other Animals
is proved to arise from the different
Quality and Quantity of Brains;
The Law of Nature is explained, as relative
to the whole Animal Creation,
The immateriality of an Inward Principle is
by Experiments and Observations exploded.

AND

A full Detail given of the several springs
which move the human machine

⟨Price one shilling⟩.

Although this was the first great age of mechanical toys, this book was not
concerned with a robot, or any variety of mechanical monster, but only
with a doctor's analysis of the human mechanism and his speculations
on the intimate relationship between mind and body. *L'Homme
machine* had been published anonymously at Leyden in 1748. Its author
was Julien Offray de La Mettrie, the son of a merchant of St. Malo, who
had qualified as a doctor of medicine in 1728 and had left France in a

hurry after puplishing a scandalous little book called 'Machiavelli's' Doctor, or the Road to Fortune for Physicians,' a satire on the medical profession, its chicanery and its money-grabbing, which the Parlement of Paris had ordered to be publicly burnt. He was also the author of *La Faculté vengée*, a ridiculous defence of the medical closed-shop which he attributed to the head of the Medical Faculty of Paris. Thus Dr La Mettrie had attacked the Faculty with one hand and defended it with the other, having his tongue in his cheek on the one occasion and stuck out at full length on the other. Little wonder that he now thought it wise to 'expatriate' himself to Leyden. The university there, La Mettrie's university, was the most modern and highly respected in Europe.

At Leyden he sat down to write *L'Homme machine*, which provoked a chorus of 'Christians of the world unite!' The doctor was now generally thought to be the enemy of mankind. As King Frederick of Prussia said, Catholic, Calvinist and Lutheran forgot for a moment their squabbles over consubstantiation, free-will, masses for the dead and the infallibility of the pope, in order to hound down a philosopher who happened to be a Frenchman. In 1745, however, the same man had published 'The Natural History of the Soul,' a rather more moderate statement of the views he was to put forward in 1748. Instead of asserting that the soul is material, or squarely denying its existence, he had limited himself to a 'sensationalism' in respect of our ideas which went no further than John Locke and the Abbé Condillac, simply showing what everyone knew, that all our thoughts and ideas are strictly conditioned by our senses, basing his argument upon his personal experience of the interaction of physical and mental health when he was a surgeon in the Regiment of Guards in the War of the Austrian Succession. 'For a philosopher an illness is a school of medicine' Frederick the Great was to say when he delivered the *éloge* at La Mettrie's death. After his experience at Dettin-gen and Fontenoy the surgeon had gone down with fever and had been led to prolonged reflection upon his own case. Here was the real spring of the themes which he embodied in *L'Homme machine*, but his earlier work, 'The Natural History of the Soul', with its chapters on the blind-ness of Dr Cheselden's patient, on teaching the deaf to speak, and on a child brought up by bears, went no further than Diderot in his *Lettre sur les aveugles*. It is true that it lost him his medical commission with the Guards, but he continued to hold various staff-posts at military hospitals. It was when he quarrelled with the doctors in addition to the priests, combining against him two of the strongest corporations of the age, that he came in for the attention of 'the double-handed engine'.

La Mettrie was the *enfant terrible* of the *Philosophes*. He was tempera¿
mentally a man to whom the strong air of controversy was the breath of
life. In *L'Homme machine* all the bravado and the impudence of his
earlier works was brought to a point and launched full in the face of the
establishment, medical and theological alike. He dedicated the book to
Albrecht von Haller, the great physiologist of Göttingen, the expert on
muscular irritability or sensitivity. Haller was noted for his pietism, his
Germanic respectability, his ponderous aversion to all materialistic
speculation. The dedication infuriated the great physiologist. He wrote
to the learned journals, disclaiming indignantly any acquaintanceship
with La Mettrie or any connection with his godless speculations. Upon
which La Mettrie published a little book called 'The Little Man with a
Long Tail', which purported to give an account of a dinner¿party at
which Haller – in the company of sundry 'nymphs' – entertained the
company with atheistical and generally improper conversation. After
this he literally fled for his life, making for Berlin where he took refuge
with Frederick the Great. At Potsdam he became Reader to the King
and a member of the Prussian Academy of the Sciences. There he wrote
L'Homme plante and other works, notably 'The Art of Happiness'. He
died there in 1751 after three days of agonising illness, as a result of
eating a tainted game¿pie. His was the death of a true *Philosophe*. Before
the machine that was La Mettrie finally ran down he was heard fre¿
quently to cry out in agony, 'Jesu! Marie!' and to the priest who
imagined him to be calling for divine assistance he rejoined: '*Mon père,
ce n'est qu'une façon de parler*'. He had once written that the fear of death
was the weakness of a child who fears ghosts and spirits, and that when
the pale messenger knocked at his door he would not find La Mettrie
afraid. 'The philosopher alone is brave when most brave men are not',
he said, game to the end in every sense.

La Mettrie's portrait tells us the truth about him, with his fat, jolly,
grinning face bursting with mischief and vitality. The epitaph beneath
it runs:'Under these lively features you may see the master of the revels,
of laughter and of *bons mots*. . . . Too daring to take care of himself . . .
he was the victim of the blockheads . . .' He might be called the buffoon
of the *Philosophe* movement. The fact that d'Alembert, the most tolerant
and kindly of his *confrères*, should have accounted it an outrage to call
him a *Philosophe* may be a measure of the man as one of the scandals of
his age. Diderot, who learnt much from him, spoke scathingly, too,
while the Marquis d'Argens called him literally a madman who wrote
like a spiritual drunkard. The title of his most notorious book is all that

is known about it by most people who talk about the *Philosophes* as mechanical materialists, contrasting their materialism unfavourably with the dialectical variety associated with the Marxists, so that it con‚ jures up something soulless, dead and barren. Goethe, who was born in the year after *L'Homme machine* was published, appears to have trans‚ ferred its mechanistic materialism to the whole encyclopedic movement. 'If we heard the Encyclopedia mentioned,' he wrote of his youth in *Dichtung und Wahrheit*, 'or opened a volume of that monstrous work, we felt as if we were going between innumerable moving spools and looms in a great factory.' Whether he ever read *L'Homme machine* is not known, but when he read the Baron d'Holbach's *Système de la nature* he thought it simply dull. 'We did not understand how such a book could be dangerous. It appeared to us so dark, so Cimmerian, so death‚like, that we found it difficult to endure it, and we shuddered at it as a spectre.' The late Sir Charles Sherrington wrongly attributes this remark to Goethe's reaction after reading *L'Homme machine*.

In point of fact, however, *L'Homme machine* is a lively and humane book. La Mettrie's whole concern with pathology indicates a liberal and reformist attitude in that age of generally illiberal and disordered institu‚ tions. Unlike the atheistical Baron d'Holbach, he does not insist that God must die. Rather he gives the impression that it would be advisable to let Him wither away from neglect. He does not deny or denounce Him. He simply says 'Don't take any notice of him', for we can know nothing about him in any case.

> How is it possible to define a being whose nature is absolutely un‚ known to us? . . . I do not here intend to call in question the existence of a supreme being; on the contrary, I am of the opinion that the greatest degree we can have of probability makes for this truth.

As for the cause of man's existence, it may be that man exists as a mush‚ room exists, thrown up by chance, without any possibility of discovering why or whence he came.

> Let us not therefore lose ourselves in infinity, since we are incapable of having the least idea of it; it is impossible for us to trace the original of things; it is a matter really indifferent to our happiness whether matter has been from all eternity, or was created; whether there is or is not a supreme being. What folly then is it to torment oneself so much in searching after what is impossible to know. What more do we know of our future destiny than we do of our original? Let us then confess our total ignorance.

An outrage to philosophy indeed! He was, d'Alembert might have said, letting the side down. After all, what were philosophers for? La Mettrie, however, simply said that to follow his agnostic advice was the way to be wise, philosophic and happy. Yet d'Alembert was right, as a *Philosophe*. For the *Philosophes'* deepest and most characteristic conviction was that all questions can be answered, including the origins of life and of man himself. And La Mettrie had declared himself a *Philosophe* who refused to try. An agnostic is the opposite of a *Philosophe*. That is why La Mettrie is not to be bracketed with d'Holbach, as Ernst Cassirer would bracket him. It is true that he is an isolated phenomenon, a special case, though not as Cassirer would say 'a retrogression into that dogmatic mode of thinking which the leading scientific minds of the eighteenth century oppose and endeavour to eliminate'.

La Mettrie claimed to derive his materialism from Descartes. He believed that Descartes had himself been a wily materialist, employing his doctrine of the dualism of the two substances, *res cogitans* and *res extensa*, as a trick to keep himself out of trouble with the Church.

> All in all, whatever he may say about the distinction of two sub stances, it is obvious that this is merely a trick and a writer's ruse, intended to make the theologians swallow a poison concealed behind an analogy.

Unfortunately Descartes lived in a bad time. 'I believe that Descartes had he been born in a more enlightened age, would have met with universal esteem . . .' Living when he did he had to dissemble. His dualism was 'a stroke of policy, a piece of finesse'. La Mettrie rejects the dualism and claims to be giving the true conclusion of Descartes's thought. The 'poisonous' possibilities of the master's work, the materialist conclusions that could be drawn from it, had long been perceived both by those who feared them and those who welcomed them. The Jesuits had long been prone to refer to Cartesian physics as 'This terrible physics, which would establish the Faith by ruining it'. The Jesuit, Denesle, in his *Examen de matérialisme* in 1754, asserted that the system of the materialists was only a step, and a perfectly natural deduction, from the physics of Descartes.

Where La Mettrie departs from Descartes, however, is in the master's 'unaccountable trespass both against our fellow creatures and against common sense' in his theory of the *bête machine*. Descartes taught that animals, or brutes (which sounds so much more derogatory) are to be distinguished from men in that while men have rational souls, animals have only corporeal souls, i.e. souls capable of all functions except cogitation, which is the norm of rationality and signalised by the use of language. This 'ruthless rupture of the traditional stair of life ranging upwards, step by step, to man', as Sherrington calls it, this lack of sym, pathy and understanding in the matter of creature kind, was a legacy from the Middle Ages when it was taught that God gave the animals to man for his own use and created them for no ends of their own. To allow the animals rational souls would involve having to admit them to heaven, and the *bête machine* was an age old prop of pious apologetics. According to Descartes man also was a machine, requiring nothing but mechanism to explain how it works, and Sherrington thought his contribution to the physiology of the nervous and motor system of man to be the greatest single contribution ever made. But of course, to Descartes man was something more, something other, than a machine. He was, so to say, a machine *plus*. His rational soul, seated in the pineal gland, distinguished him from all other machines. This notion La Mettrie could not accept. 'The soul . . . is nothing but an empty term', he writes, 'of which we have no idea, and which a man of right understanding ought to make use of to express only that part of us which thinks.' The faculties of the soul depend so much upon the proper organisation of the brain, and indeed of the whole body, that they appear to be nothing but this organisation itself. The body soul mechanism may best be called an enlightened machine.

All this, says La Mettrie, is pefectly obvious to a physician. Indeed, he is the best physician who has the greatest knowledge of the mechanical constitution of the human body, and 'who does not trouble himself about the soul, nor all that train of perplexities which this chimera is apt to raise in foolish ignorant brains . . .' If he is asked what makes the brutes differ from us, he answers that the distinction is one of organisation only. A man has more springs, wheels, etc., than a monkey, just as Vaucanson's mechanical flute player had more than his mechanical duck. Animals (brutes) could be men if they had a few more 'works'. It is only more and better organisation that would serve to make animals into men. Nature made us all of the same paste, and the other animals want only a higher degree of fermentation to make them equal to man in everything. They must, therefore, partake – after their kind – in the prerogatives of human kind. La Mettrie thus remedied the 'unaccountable trespass' committed by Descartes against our fellow creatures and against common sense. He mended the staircase, and in so doing was on the track of something like a modern theory of evolution. He sees no reason why selected animals should not be taught to talk. Even Mr Locke had not been surprised at the vocal qualities of parrots. Why not baboons, creatures so near to man in structure? A carefully selected baboon could be educated under a good tutor.

> I would choose one with the most sensible face. . . . Then he would no longer be a wild or imperfect man; he would be a complete man, a polite little fellow, with as many members and muscles as ourselves, to think and improve with his education.

There is a mystery here, but we may suppose that the whole difference between man and the other animals is produced by physical causes, even if we cannot yet follow out these causes in the way they have their effects.

Diversity of organisation accounts not only for the differences between man and the other animals, but for the inequalities between different men and women. Diderot and La Mettrie shared this organisational theory of differentiation. It singles them out from the 'education-mad' school who preferred to believe that all men can be made equal in abilities and powers by uniform education, in other words that '*L'éduca- tion peut tout*'. This is the most important division within the *Philosophes*, the division between those who give primary importance to nature, and those who give it to nurture. La Mettrie thought that ethical writers had been wrong to rank as valuable only those qualities or talents which are acquired by reflection, industry, education. They should rank equally highly those 'which we receive directly from Nature'. Whence, he asks, come skill, science and virtue, but from a *disposition* that renders us proper to become skilful, knowing and virtuous? He thinks 'we ought to esteem a superior disposition, or organisation, and be proud of it, not apologetic: not try to explain it away by talk of environment'. Education is the *second* most important factor: organisation is the source of all. Nature first, nurture second.

> The best framed brain without education would be to no purpose, as without the knowledge of the world the best made man would be but a gross peasant. . . . What would the very best school avail without a matrix perfectly open for the entrance or conception of ideas?

Ten years before Helvétius wrote *De l'esprit* La Mettrie had refuted it. He was dead in 1758, but Diderot answered *De l'esprit*, on the La Mettrie basis, in his *Réfutation suivie de l'ouvrage d'Helvétius intitulé l'Homme*. The psychologists either lacked, or ignored, the evidence of the physical sciences – the natural history of the century. This it is which prevents any but the superficial student from lumping Diderot and La Mettrie together with the *Philosophes* in general as mechanical, sensationalist environmentalists.

> How shall we ever investigate the hidden causes of the endless variety of human minds? They would escape the eyes of a lynx or of an argus. A mere nothing, a minute fibre, something too subtle for the nicest anatomy, would have made two dunces of Erasmus and Fontenelle.

The passage sums up his deep and constant appreciation of the infinite variety of human beings, and suggests that Diderot was right when he spoke of the cogency of a man's thinking depending on his being an anatomist, a physiologist, a naturalist and a physician. It was high time that a doctor of medicine became a *Philosophe*. For one thing it would teach a man not to be a snob about materialism, or about other animals than himself. La Mettrie was proud of the antiquity of materialism. ' 'Tis not behaving like a philosopher', he wrote, 'to blush with Pliny at the misery of our origin . . . Matter has nothing contemptible in it, tho' it may appear so to coarse eyes.' Nor is there any reason why man should look down on the brutes. 'Man is framed of materials not exceeding in value those of other animals; nature has made us of one and the same paste, she has only diversified the ferment in working it up.' This is the essential democracy of the materialist.

There is an admirable simplicity and straightforwardness about the author of *L'Homme machine*. This comes out at the beginning when he states his dissatisfaction with Locke. Locke had raised the question whether matter can think, but La Mettrie considered that to ask such a question was as illegitimate as to ask whether matter can tell the time. 'It is not matter, as such, that can tell the time: it is a clock, matter organised in a certain way, that can do that.' Nor will he leave us in any doubt about man the machine. 'Let us conclude boldly then that man is a machine; and that there is only one substance, differently modified, in the whole universe.' Man is a material unity: a clock that winds up its own springs, a living image of perpetual motion. How does it do this? By assimilation operating on organisation, and vice versa. Much of the opening part of the work is devoted to the part played in this process by nutriment and assimilation, the interplay of mind and body. In both his life and his death La Mettrie showed himself to be a typical Frenchman with regard to food.

> What a vast power there is in a repast! Joy revives in a disconsolate heart; it is transfused into the souls of all the guests, who express it by amiable conversation and music.

The English are a proud and fierce race. They like their steaks under-done. A hanging judge becomes humane after a good meal. 'It is much to be wished that we had none for judges but the most skilful physicians. They alone could distinguish the guilty from the innocent . . .' The basis for a more humane and constructive attitude to crime and punishment is not so much the attempt to remake the human race by re-education, but rather an efficient public-health service, along with plentiful and nourishing food. 'This is my system, or rather this is the truth, if I am not much mistaken. It is short and plain. Let who will dispute it.'

Chapter Ten

THE CRITICAL DECADE

*I do not know whether I have too good an opinion of my century;
but it seems to me that there is a certain fermentation of universal
reason.*

CHARLES PINOT DUCLOS

THE central decade of the eighteenth century was the turning point of
the *ancien régime* in France. As d'Alembert said in his *Éléments de
philosphie*, the mid‑point of the century was as usual the critical time of
transition. In the fifteenth century the Italian Renaissance had begun in
the middle years; the Reformation had begun in the middle years of the
sixteenth; the Cartesian revolution in philosophy began somewhere
between 1629 and 1649. That the eighteenth century was able justly to
call itself the century of philosophy *par excellence* was the achievement
of the central years, though it was in fact the century of the *popularisation*
of philosophy at the hands of the *Philosophes*. On entering the French
Academy in 1787, the historian Claude de Rulhière was to look back to
1749 as the beginning of the revolution in France, when Paris lost its
deference for the opinions and tastes of the Court and there arose
'the empire of public opinion'. The *gens de lettres* were the organs, the
arbiters, of this change, when the desire to instruct took precedence over
the desire to please, the philosopher over the libertine, Diderot and the
Encyclopedists over Fontenelle. 'People are talking of nothing but the
necessity of an early revolution', wrote the Marquis d'Argenson,
'because of the bad conditions in which the government finds itself in‑
ternally.' Voltaire, looking back over fifteen years from 1767, said much
the same. The revolution had already taken place in men's minds, and
'the cries of the pedants herald this great change as the croaking of
ravens herald good weather'. In that very year, 1749, Rulhière pointed
out, 'were produced all these great philosophical works', and indeed the
concentration of philosophical talent at that point in time is remarkable.
But if what Charles Pinot Duclos in 1750 called '*une . . . fermentation de*

raison universelle' were to produce real progress it needed direction by *'une éducation bien étendue'*. It was such an extensive education that the great Encyclopedia provided. Its *Discours préliminaire* and the first vol‹ ume appeared in the next year, 1751.

1749 was the year when France made the Treaty of Aix‹la‹Chapelle. At Fontenoy she had enjoyed the last glorious victory of the *ancien régime*, but d'Argenson failed to reap any real advantage from it, and he was dismissed in 1747. When his successor, Maurice de Saxe, engin‹ eered the treaty of Aix two years later, France gained nothing. The peace with England provided for the mutual restoration of conquests, and Louis XV was left with the heavy burden of paying for an unprofitable war while the English proceeded with their conquests in North America, something which interested France a good deal less than recovering her own waning dominance on the continent of Europe. From this point France entered upon the slippery slope of diplomatic and military failure which reached its culmination in the Seven Years War. Reform at home, made the more urgent by the expense of the War of the Austrian Succession, was initiated by the financial expedients of Machault d'Arnouville, the new Controller‹General. In 1749 he brought in the *vingtième*, a tax of one‹twentieth of all incomes, including those of the noblesse and clergy. Louis XV had to compel the Parlements and the provincial estates to register the edict, seeking as it did for the first time seriously to extend the incidence of taxation to the privileged classes. By 1751 the attempt had failed, and by 1759 things were worse than ever, Frederick the Great winning at Rossbach and the English at Minden, Quebec and Quiberon Bay. Seven volumes of the Encyclopedia were out, and so was Helvétius's *De l'esprit* and Voltaire's *Candide*. There had even been an attempt on the life of the king. Everything had been going wrong for France for a decade, the decade of the enlightenment. It seemed that national loss and humiliation went hand in hand with the triumphs of the *nouvelle façon commune de penser*. Putting two and two together it seemed that the country was paying too heavily for the privilege of leading the world in liberal philosophy. The licence for publishing the Encyclopedia was revoked in the spring of 1759.

The suppression of 1759 was only temporary. The decade 1749–59 was to prove in retrospect the flowering‹time of the modern mind. The battle for the mind of France was fought and won by the men of letters in these years, and the *Philosophes* were in the middle of the scene. Their work engaged all minds, for they were literally 'the talk of the town'. It was incredible, as M. de Castries said, that 'people don't talk of anything but these fellows. Persons without an establishment, who don't have a house, who are lodged in a garret . . . One just can't get used to it.' No inconsiderable part of their success was owing to their critics and enemies. When Jacob,Nicolas Moreau put forth his *Avis utile* against them in 1757 he called them a tribe of savages whose 'Whole substance is nothing but venom and corruption. The source of it', he said, 'is inexhaustible and is always flowing.' They hoarded their venom beneath their tongues and shot it at their enemies from behind. Moreau christened them the tribe of the *Cacouacs*, and the name stuck. It was in its perverse way something of a tribute. In the same year Palissot published his *Petites Lettres sur les grands philosophes*, directed in the first instance against d'Alembert. It charged the Encyclopedists with servile imitation of Francis Bacon, and with having impudently monopolised the name of philosophers. 'All these gentlemen call themselves philosophers,' Palissot remarked. 'Some of them are.' His play, *Les Philosophes*, put them on the Parisian stage in 1760 with special attention to Diderot and Rousseau, who was shown in pursuit of a lettuce. It was a poor thing as a play, of purely topical and ephemeral interest, but once again, even if trivially, the *Philosophes* occupied the centre of the scene.

It is important not to suppose, for all the manœuvres of their enemies, that the *Philosophes* were monopolists of the intellectual scene in these years. There were three factions in the French intellectual scene in the first half of the eighteenth century, each with its own Academy. There were *les beaux,esprits*, or the wits, who belonged to the Académie Française. There were the *érudits*, or the antiquarians, who frequented the Académie des Inscriptions. The *Philosophes* belonged generally to the Académie des Sciences, and were proud to be 'moderns'. The an, tagonism between the two last was really the latest phase of the old contest between the Ancients and the Moderns. The Académie des Sciences, self,consciously on the side of progress and the future, ac, counted itself the top,ranking body and held the Académie des Inscrip, tions in some contempt, with its emphasis on 'mere memory', as Montes, quieu had held it in his *Lettres persanes*, writing as he was from the angle of the *Philosophes* at the time. Edward Gibbon, arriving in Paris in 1763, and finding the term *érudit* used of such scholars as Casaubon and Montfaucon as a term of disdain, was deeply shocked, and wrote his *Essai sur l'étude de la littérature* in 1765 as a reproof to d'Alembert who maintained the attitude in his *Discours préliminaire*. D'Alembert had made it clear that he held them for pedants whose sole merit (if a merit it was) consisted of an indiscriminate collection of facts.

But the *érudits* came in for abuse at other hands than those of d'Alembert. For example, the painter Chardin had ridiculed them in his picture
of *Le Singe antiquaire* in the Salon of 1740. Monkeys were all the fashion
for satirical attack on the imitative artist at this time, as may be seen
from the work of Watteau and the younger Teniers. *Le Singe antiquaire*
showed a monkey surrounded by antique *objets d'art*, examining a
medal through a magnifying-glass, and bearing the legend: 'Why worry
about antique objects? Our century, to really philosophic eyes, offers
enough matter for contemplation.' Diderot himself loved the antique,
but he wrote a fragment called *Anticomanie* to ridicule those who admired the antique simply because it was antique, without discriminating
between what was ancient and beautiful and what was simply ancient.
The *Philosophes* called the *érudits* 'the execrable race of *érudits*', and the
érudits returned the compliment by describing the *Philosophes* as 'drolls
and sectaries'. Both indulged in a good deal of in-fighting, and what they
said to each other was often true. The gulf between them in France was
a real one. Jean Seznec rightly insists that their antagonism was 'not a
conflict of political or religious ideas . . . but partly social antagonism.'
The head of the *érudits*, the Comte de Caylus, was a grand seigneur and
looked down on 'these pen men, these scribblers who are in the process
of becoming so powerful, and are perhaps on the point of supplanting
the nobility.' Above all, he emphasises, what divided the two was 'a
difference of imagination'. May it not be that Caylus wished to recapture
the ancient world as a whole, while Diderot, like a true *Philosophe*,
wished to make a selective use of it for the purpose of the present? In
other words, Diderot approached it, like everything else, as *un homme
engagé*? Caylus, the old *collectionneur*, wishes his mortal remains to be
placed in an ancient urn. Upon which Diderot composed the epitaph:

> *Ci-gît un antiquaire acariâtre et brusque.*
> *Oh qu'il est bien logé dans cette cruche étrusque!* [1]

'I know little about Diderot, for I hold him in no esteem,' said Caylus.
'However, I believe he is very well. Some buggers never die.' Madame
Geoffrin respected their differences by inviting them to attend her salon
on different evenings: Mondays and Wednesdays respectively. Gibbon
tried in vain to bring them together, but he reconciled them in his own
person. 'He is the perfect blend of the philosopher and the antiquarian',
writes Momigliano in his essay on Gibbon's contribution to historical

---

[1] 'Here lies a brusque and peevish antiquarian. How properly he is lodged in this
ancient jug!'

method. As an English visitor he did not feel compelled to join in the bitter faction-fighting of the French. The nearest to a detached observer among the French intellectuals of the mid-century was perhaps Duclos, and he continued to oppose the admission of Diderot to the Academié Française because he held him to be a sectary and a fanatic. In his *Considérations* he refused to equate the *Philosophes* with the *gens d'esprit* who composed the Academy.

PART III
The Encyclopedia

Chapter Eleven

TO CHANGE THE COMMON
MANNER OF THINKING

... le caractère que doit avoir un bon dictionnaire, le caractère est
de changer la façon commune de penser.

DIDEROT

THUS Diderot was, as they say, 'short' on Academies. He became a
Member of the Royal Prussian Academy of Sciences and Belles-Lettres
in 1751, just in time for the fact to be advertised on the title-page of the
first volume of the Encyclopedia, and he was later to become a member of
two Societies in Russia and of the Society of Antiquaries of Scotland, but
he was never admitted to any learned society in France. It is hardly
surprising that the Royal Society of London shunned him after the
Saunderson episode in the *Lettre sur les aveugles*. The cutler's son was
a kind of rogue journalist of genius, and a garret-dwelling Parisian hack
who lived by translating English books and composing sermons for the
priests of a religion he did not believe in, and in the winter of 1749 he
was just out of prison. How did such a man become the leading figure in
what was to be a great national enterprise? There was, of course, a certain
amount of chance about it. The translator of Dr James's *Medical
Dictionary* was invited to do the *Cyclopedia* of Ephraim Chambers, and
this was expanded into a national Encyclopedia largely in consequence
of Diderot's negotiations with the associated booksellers of Paris. The
initiative always came from the trade, for the Encyclopedia – fortunately
for its success – was first and last a business enterprise. Diderot was the
best-regarded journeyman for the task, and he knew everyone in his own
line of business. He could recruit the necessary team of translators, for
translation of the English contributors to Chambers's work promised to
be the bulk of the work involved. Ninety-five articles were lifted from
Chambers straight away.

Then there was the man's charm, his conquering vivacity. The leading publisher, Le Breton, had originally contracted for the work with an Englishman, John Mills, and had quarrelled with him, indeed come to blows with him. The original contract had to be cancelled with the assistance of the Chancellor, the elderly and pious d'Arguesseau. Diderot met the Chancellor and charmed him with his enthusiasm and his uninhibited eloquence almost precisely at the time of his own denuncia‑ tion to the police as a dangerous freethinker: *Un garçon plein d'esprit, mais extrêmement dangereux*, so the police had him down in their records, 'a bright lad, but extremely dangerous'. A hack translator, a writer of pornography, a deist on the way to becoming an atheist, an old inhabitant of His Majesty's fortress of Vincennes: it was fortunate that the great enterprise passed into the hands of a man of such persistent unorthodoxy, such chastening experience of the powers that be, such barometric response to the intellectual currents of the age as the man of Langres. He was a great Frenchman and was intent on the work becoming a veritable monument to the genius of his country and his age. 'My plan is to do something never before attempted', he told Le Breton. 'Our Encyclopedia will be not only the best work of its kind, but the greatest collaborative intellectual enterprise in the history of man, a synthesis of the French genius, the monument of our century.' The words are typical of the man, and they are prophetically true.

The work could not be achieved without *le privilège du roi*, the official imprimatur. Not only the royal licence was obtained, but the King's Printer. It is these facts that justify the description of the Encyclopedia as the 'Trojan Horse' of the *ancien régime*. It had to be directed to the solid and respectable middle‑class reader, the only public which could be depended upon to subscribe the sum of sixty livres and to continue a subscription of twenty‑four livres per volume, after the first, for seven‑ teen volumes, not to mention the expensive volumes of plates. For these sums the reader would receive some 20 million words over some fourteen years. A thousand subscribers were enrolled within six months of the issue of the prospectus, and there were at least four thousand in the end. The demand extended to the Western world in general, the booksellers of France coming to an arrangement with the English when the pirates announced a half‑price edition after the first volume. The work proved an immense asset to the export trade, to the native printing industry, and to the national cult of *la gloire*. This last fact is generally neglected when historians reminisce upon the failures and humiliations of France towards the end of the *ancien régime*. Nor is it sufficiently remembered, in recounting the crises through which the enterprise passed, that France could not afford to allow it to fail or to pass into other hands. The wide[,]spread 'vested interest' in the Encyclopedia also helps to account for the the fact that it is, above all other such works, vastly entertaining. It had to be in order to keep its subscribers happy. There was about it a good deal of what novelists call *le progrès d'effet*. One never could be sure what the next volume of the Encyclopedia would contain, and, while it hardly held people as the numbers of *The Pickwick Papers* did, it certainly held them.

The exigencies of salesmanship played an important part in deter[,]mining the tone and content of the volumes. Criticism of the establish[,]ment had to be oblique in view of the quasi-official character of the undertaking. This is one consideration which makes Voltaire's com[,]plaints of its timidity unreasonable. The editors and the printers did their work not on the Swiss frontier or in Holland, but in the capital of France. Like so much of the work of the *Philosophes*, from Fontenelle onwards, it was done under the noses of the powers that be, and perhaps more importantly under those of the literate middle class whose 'manner of thinking' it was intended to change or to modify. The tactics of evasion are in evidence from the beginning. For example, the Abbé Mallet's article on ARC in volume one supplies a perfectly serious account of the dimensions of Noah's floating home, reflecting without undue scepticism upon the problems of accommodation for the extensive ranks of the animal creation, concluding gravely, 'the Word of God, who has explained himself positively on these important matters leaves no room for hypothesis'. These are the difficulties which confront Christians in the somewhat contradictory biblical accounts of these things, and 'no conclusions are drawn, either about the truth of religion, or about the sincerity of the authors of sacred history'. It is difficult to see what exception could be taken to this, even when it is pointed out that there is a difference between the truths of religion and the truths of history, be[,]tween the certainty of a fact and the sincerity of the man who recounts it.

Similarly there is from the beginning a plenitude of attention to the useful arts, or *métiers*, a certain concentration upon the practical affairs of practical men. The tone could be set at once in a volume containing under 'A' such subjects as ACIER (steel), AIGUILLES (needles) and ARGENT (silver). Much of the 'leg-work' involved in seeking out the right people prepared to supply the right information on the industrial processes involved here was done by Diderot personally. The cutler's son, coming from the French version of Sheffield in those days, was to be relied upon for anything to do with the metallurgical trades. 'ARMORIAL

BEARINGS', too, came in volume one, 'a vain and ridiculous science' on which the book⸝trade flourished while lacking a single pamphlet on shirt, stocking and shoe⸝making. The Encyclopedia was to include an illustrated account of the rural craft of sabot⸝making.

Volume one contains also two other examples of the evasive technique. One was the hiding of dangerous matter in unlikely places, something that must have at once disconcerted and entertained orthodox sub⸝scribers. Under ACIUS LOCUTIUS (the Roman god of speech, an obscure pagan deity) was planted a plea for freedom of speech in a proposal that criticism of the Church and Government should only be permitted in what Gibbon calls 'the decent obscurity of a learned language', thus reconciling freedom of thought with respect for the people's faith and 'the national cult'. Another example of the same tactic is contained in the article on AIGLE, which is not in the least ornithological, but contrasts the benighted pagans and their superstitions with the Christians who are called upon to believe only 'fine, sublime and holy Things'. In our religion, it is announced, we have only to follow reason in order to arrive 'at the foot of the altar'. The other characteristic is a certain pedantic solemnity which arrives at sheer comedy. The Aguapa tree is disposed of in a few lines which declare that if those who live near it do not know more about it than we do, woe betide them; while the Aguaxima plant of Brazil is said to be included simply because it would have been improper to leave it out. There is as much of Montaigne and Rabelais about the Encyclopedia as there is of Ephraim Chambers. Volume one also contained a lengthy article on AUTORITÉ POLITIQUE which was once thought to have been written by Rousseau. It was attacked by the Jesuit *Journal de Trévoux* as derived from a seditious essay by Daniel Defoe called 'Judgment of the Whole Kingdoms and Nations concerning the Rights, Powers and Prerogatives of Kings' 1710, though in the *Errata pour les deux premiers volumes* it was denied that its author had ever seen the article in question. Anyone sampling the Encyclopedia by dipping into the first volume can find examples of almost all its features as a whole.

What the work professed to be had been laid down in the prospectus of 1750, and from it can be gathered what were considered to be the principal shortcomings of Chambers, apart from history, biography and the mechanical arts. It was to be a genuine philosophic picture of the human mind in all ages and all places. The emphasis was laid upon integration; not merely the presentation of a vast accumulation of knowledge, but the exhibition of *l'enchaînement des connaissances*, and indicating 'the connection, near and remote, of the beings that compose nature'. If this were to be achieved effectively, revealing the intertwining of the roots and branches of all the various kinds of knowledge, thus completing 'a circle of knowledge', it would be essential to depart from the alphabetical arrangement of Chambers. The prospectus, with all the optimistic aplomb of Diderot, undertook to do just this, and in order to sketch out the pattern of the *enchaînement* there was folded into the prospectus a chart or *schema* based on that drawn up by Bacon (under the head, 'Survey of the Intellectual Globe') for his *Advancement of Learning*. To the *Philosophes*, Bacon was the first person in the trinity of English philosophy, along with Newton and Locke. There were three Faculties, 'MEMORY' 'REASON' and 'IMAGINATION', each with its relevant branch of science, 'HISTORY', 'PHILOSOPHY' and 'POETRY'. The way the various sub-divisions are ranged under these three reveals at once the psychological warfare that was intended. There is a visual and organic relation between 'PHILOSOPHY' and 'REASON'. 'PHILOSOPHY' is divided into SCIENCE DE LA NATURE, SCIENCE DE L'HOMME and SCIENCE DE DIEU. Under the latter heading, in which God is dignified with full capitals, are set out 'THEOLOGY' and 'RELIGION' in a diminutive space, hardly occupying a deeper column than iron-manufacture.

It was doubtless very well for Bacon, who never produced an encyclo-pedia, to lay down this *scheme*, but when it came to producing an encyclo-pedic work in seventeen volumes it had to be abandoned almost at once. The only practical way for an editor working with a vast team of con-tributors and producing the work volume by volume over the years was to have recourse to the despised alphabetical order of Chambers. Having boasted of the *enchaînement des connaissances* as indicated in the *schema* it proved necessary to begin at A and go on to B and C, volume by volume. Having expressed dissatisfaction with the Chambers model of a mere 'dictionary of definitions' arranged alphabetically it was necessary to have recourse to it, even if the result were to be something better than a dictionary of definitions. The compromise is expressed in the sub-title: '*dictionnaire raisonné*'. The adjective *raisonné* indicated the *enchaînement*, the system of cross-reference which would bring out the internal order of the work, the boasted 'intertwining' of the roots and branches of knowledge. The alphabetical method of presentation is defended in the closing paragraph of the prospectus thus:

> If it is objected that an alphabetical order destroys the internal connec-
> tion of our system of human knowledge, we answer that the internal
> connection consists less in the arrangement of the materials than in the
> bearings they have upon each other; nothing can destroy these, and

we shall take care to render them apparent by the arrangement of the material comprising each article and by the precision and frequency of the cross-references [*renvois*].

These much-boasted *renvois* were to have the technical function of bringing out the *enchaînement* which was the essential feature of 'a circle of knowledges'. The underlying hope was that the *enchaînement* thus contrived and revealed would serve to discredit the irrational element in an alphabetical arrangement of knowledge, so that no one part (e.g. the theological) should stand immune from the criticism afforded by the rest (the sciences of nature, etc.), the whole operating for the cause of universal reason and thereby changing the common manner of thinking, which was the whole purpose of the work. In the article on ENCYCLOPÉDIE which Diderot wrote under E he made it plain that he was using the technique of the *renvoi* explicitly for the purpose of propagating the truth. Having justified the *renvois* for the purpose of *enchaînement*, 'to give the whole that unity which is so favourable to the establishment and conviction of truth', he proclaimed their critical purpose of bringing ideas and principles into opposition. It is thus that they attack, shake, overturn 'secretly certain ridiculous opinions which one dare not attack openly'. In this remarkably frank article he openly explains the critical value of the *renvois* in the phrase quoted at the head of this chapter: 'They give the Encyclopedia the character that a good dictionary should have; this character is to change the common manner of thinking.' A dictionary, as G. K. Chesterton once said, is the most tendentious book in the world. Certainly this one was.

Despite all this, the *renvois* were not used in the event as frequently or as effectively as they might have been. It is important not to overstate the frequency of their use. The best-known example is perhaps under CORDELIER (the Franciscan greyfriars), which begins with seven lines of straight definition taken out of Chambers, followed by eight lines of tendentious comment, culminating in four lines of scathing irony. Then comes the *renvoi* to CAPUCHON. Turning up CAPUCHON one comes upon the 'poison' and a *renvoi* back to CORDELIER.

Chapter Twelve

DISCOURS PRÉLIMINAIRE

DIDEROT'S prospectus of November 1750 tells us much of the character of the *Encyclopédie*, its scope and its technique of presentation, but for the manifesto of the mind which it was to represent and express we must turn to d'Alembert's *Discours préliminaire* which introduced the first volume. D'Alembert is given his full titles on the frontispiece: he is described as '*de l'Académie Royal des Sciences de Paris, de celle de Prusse, et de la Societé Royale de Londres*'. It is an impressive array, and the *Discours préliminaire* is worthy of d'Alembert's credentials. As Frederick the Great wrote to its author: 'Many have won battles and conquered pro, vinces, but few have written a work as perfect as the preface to the Encyclopedia', and when Condorcet delivered the *éloge* to his master and fellow-mathematician in 1784 he singled out the *Discours* as one of the two or three priceless works of the century. It has ever since been regarded as 'the best summary of the mind of the eighteenth century'. Unlike Condorcet's famous *Esquisse*, which was composed in the shadow of the guillotine, the *Discours* owed little of its economy to time's winged chariot. It was the product of a confident and hopeful intellect at the height of its powers. D'Alembert was in his early forties, past his zenith as a mathematician, and perfectly situated for the exploration and expression of the mind of his age. He still has some of the impatience of a young man, but he is beyond the worst excesses of dogmatism or the superstitions of the 'Progressive'.

The *Discours* has been called the *Essay on Method* of the Enlighten, ment. That title would apply better to Diderot's *Pensées sur l'interpréta, tion de la nature*, with its attempt to make a synthesis of the methods of Newton and Descartes. D'Alembert in the *Discours* is not recommend, ing a certain technique of thinking, a procedure. He is introducing an encyclopedia by sketching a picture of the *connaissances* in their hierarchy and their inter-relations, and then by a brief description of the progress of philosophy in modern times. These sections are followed by a justification for dictionaries in general and this one in particular, with a critical appreciation of Chambers's work, and an explanation of the recourse to alphabetical arrangement. The *Discours* ends with a few pages of acknow‹ ledgement to the contributors which amount to a detailed treatment of what Diderot had merely indicated in the prospectus. This final section is in fact a rewriting and expansion of what Diderot had already done in the brief terms of an advertisement. What the *Philosophes* thought about their age, what they thought about the nature of knowledge, may be gathered from such a survey, but d'Alembert might have said of it what he said about the Encyclopedists in general: people would know how to judge what they thought as distinct from what they said.

Perhaps the most remarkable feature of his sketch of modern intellec‹ tual history is his omission of Pierre Bayle, whose Dictionary was an inspiration and quarry for the Encyclopedists.[1] Is it possible that the great sceptic was too dangerous for inclusion in a *Discours* addressed to the subscribers the editors had in mind? It is worth noting, too, the sober care with which d'Alembert handles the question of scholarly scruple, appropriate to a scholar of his credentials. After all, his member‹ ship of the learned societies was regarded as an invaluable asset in further‹ ing the intellectual respectability of the work. Not only does he boast of the clear and precise use of sources, but he asks the reader to believe that the authors have not only refused to protect 'discarded opinions uncritically' but have refused to prescribe 'accepted opinions without reason'. As for 'our enlightened age', which the *Philosophes* were (and are) accused of boosting uncritically, d'Alembert has some surprisingly acid things to say: 'Barbarism lasts for centuries; it seems that it is our natural element; reason and good taste are only passing.' He is par‹ ticularly concerned that 'the philosophic spirit so much in fashion today which tried to comprehend everything and to take nothing for granted, was extending even into belles‹lettres'. He deplores the way men now use terms like 'the anatomy of the soul', the way they make dissertations instead of conversing, so that 'our societies have lost their principal ornaments – warmth and gaiety'. A sad reflection at the mid‹century by the blithe and smiling Jean le Rond, and very difficult to believe of France at any time. He was well enough aware, however, that science had benefited, in terms of popularity at least, by the invasion of scientific books by the tone and style previously associated with belles‹lettres. He cites both Fontenelle and Buffon here, and with approval.

It is important to realise that the *Philosophes* indulged only in a qualified pride in the triumph of philosophy in their age. Indeed,

[1] See above, pp. 32-5.

d'Alembert remarks that philosophy, which constitutes 'the dominant taste of our century', seems to be trying to make up for the time it has lost. Locke, who in retrospect seems to have dominated the Enlighten‹ ment in France, is regarded by d'Alembert as 'finally beginning to have some readers and a few partisans among us'. The delayed action of great thinkers, he suggests, is in part due to the practice today of writing everything in the vulgar tongue instead of in Latin, so that before long it will be necessary for an educated man 'to burden his memory with seven or eight different languages. And after having consumed the most precious time of his life in learning them, he will die before beginning to silence himself.' D'Alembert hopes despondently, for a return to Latin usage, although he is willing to concede that the practice of writing in French had contributed to making enlightenment more general. He seems to think that his countrymen, while 'singularly eager for novelties in matters of taste', were far too much 'attached to ancient opinions in matters of science'. Newton had demolished the Cartesian physics almost before the French had considered adopting them. 'Twenty years have not yet passed since we began to renounce Cartesianism in France.' Sticking to Descartes had become almost a matter of national pride. D'Alembert suffers from a typical French ambivalence in his attitude to the English here. On the one hand he will say that 'England is indebted to us for the origins of the philosophy which we have since received back from her'. On the other, he shares the usual habit of the *Philosophes* since Voltaire in holding up England's liberal virtues in order to contrast the attachment of France to the deplorable abuses of the *ancien régime*. Newton's philosophy, for instance, had been generally accepted by his countrymen in his lifetime 'because he was dealing with a nation that was less unjust than others'. D'Alembert obviously shared in what was at that time called the French *anglomanie*.

D'Alembert, in the third section of his *Discours*, gives the typically 'loaded' account of intellectual history. The masterpieces of the ancients in almost all genres were 'forgotten for twelve centuries', and even at the Renaissance men believed that the only way to imitate the ancients was to copy them slavishly. When he deals with the Renaissance it is only with France that he deals, going on rapidly to Malherbe, Corneille and Racine, with a very brief reference to Italy. The Middle Ages were a waste of time. 'Scholasticism, which constituted the whole of so‹called science in the centuries of ignorance' is ignored and only treated as 'prejudicial to the progress of true philosophy in that first century [the seventeenth] of enlightenment'. The world begins anew with 'the immortal Chancellor of England'. Francis Bacon one is tempted to regard as 'the greatest, the most universal, and the most eloquent of the philosophers'. Yet d'Alembert's admiration gives the impression of being born rather of astonishment than of understanding, a fate that Bacon was to suffer frequently in modern times; appreciation for the wrong reasons. Coleridge was to maintain the tradition by admiring the great empiricist as a Platonist. D'Alembert appears to admire him as a brilliant phenomenon flashing across an age of darkness. 'Born in the depth of the most profound night', he says, as if he were talking about Francis's namesake, Roger, in the thirteenth century. He wishes to adopt the immortal Chancellor's 'Tree' of knowledge even while he insists on modifying it in certain respects, chiefly, one suspects, in order to counter the charge of the enemies of the Encyclopedists that their work was a wholesale plagiarism.

> We have in certain respects pushed the subdivisions [of the sciences] further, especially in the parts on mathematics and on particular physics. On the other hand, we have abstained from extending as far as he does the subdivision of certain sciences, which he follows to the last twigs of their branches.

Both Bacon's 'Tree' and the Encyclopedic variation are printed.

The influence of Bacon is consistently overstated. In fact the *Philosophes* of the Encyclopedia were a good deal closer to Descartes. Bacon, the great champion of the inductive method and of a rigorous empiricism, was in many respects alien. As a geometer, d'Alembert finds Descartes with his 'sublime geometry' incomparable. He carried the rationalist cult of simplicity and unity into his work as a *Philosophe*, as a mathe‹ matician might be expected to do. The simplicity of all the great prin‹ ciples of knowledge was the fruit of the 'geometrical spirit', as was the celebrated *enchaînement* of the *connaissances*, whereas the vast catalogue of the sciences with their almost infinite subdivisions in Bacon's 'Tree' was nothing but a collection, and if they had any *enchaînement* it was imposed externally. The adoption of Bacon as the presiding spirit of the *Discours* while Descartes is treated secondarily, almost left‹handedly, is the paradox of the whole exercise. Having given Descartes his due for his immortal work in applying algebra to geometry, and for his 'most profound investigations . . . in all the physico‹mathematical sciences', he goes on to suggest that 'as a philosopher he was perhaps equally great, but he was not so fortunate'. As for the 'attractive theory' of the vortices, it has become almost ridiculous, although we must allow that 'at that time nothing better could be imagined'. It was 'one of the finest and most ingenious hypotheses that philosophy has ever imagined'. Yet, after all, it was but a hypothesis. The best that can be said is that if it has proved wrong, perhaps we had to pass by way of the vortices in order to arrive at a true system of the world. Descartes is best thought of as 'a leader of conspirators, daring to show intelligent minds how to throw off the yoke of scholasticism'. If he concluded by believing he could explain everything, he at least began by doubting everything, and the arms which we use to combat him belong to him no less because we turn them against him . . . 'Above all let us not confound his cause by that of his sectaries.' Nothing shows more clearly than this kind of remark the embarrassment of Descartes to the *Philosophes*, since the orthodox had succeeded in canonising him, even though his works had been on the Index since 1663, and in 1667 the Chancellor of the University of Paris had been forbidden by royal order to deliver an *éloge* on the occasion of his burial in the soil of France. One might have imagined that this was sufficient to preserve him as patron-saint of the *Philosophes*.

'Our own century will leave monuments to posterity for which it may rightfully glorify itself.' Towards the end of the second section of the *Discours*, d'Alembert celebrates the rare genius of Voltaire and of Montesquieu, who is 'as good a citizen as he is a great philosopher'. He does his best to speak up for Rousseau as well, but he confesses that it would ill become the Encyclopedia to concur with the thrusts of a writer, however eloquent and philosophical, who accuses the arts and sciences of corrupting human mores. 'We will not reproach him for having con-fused the cultivation of the mind with the abuse that can be made of it.' Nothing that the gentle Jean le Rond could say, however, could arrest the deterioration of the relations between the *Philosophes* and the irascible Jean-Jacques. The article which d'Alembert wrote on Geneva for volume seven, and Rousseau's reply in his *Lettre à d'Alembert*, were to make the breach complete.

In the final section of the *Discours* where d'Alembert largely rewrote Diderot's prospectus, he was to relate the Encyclopedia to previous attempts in the same vein, and especially to the *Cyclopedia* of Ephraim Chambers. He fends off the charge that was frequently to be made, that the Encyclopedists had lifted much of their work from the English pro-ject, with the counterblast that 'perhaps Chambers would never have seen the light of day in English if in our own language there had not already existed the works from which Chambers indiscriminately and impru-dently drew most of the things that went into his dictionary'. A simple translation of Chambers would have excited the indignation of scholars at finding themselves presented, under a new and ostentatious title, with what they already possessed. He also shows the inadequacy of Chambers in its treatment of the liberal arts, and its total deficiency in the mechan‑ ical arts. 'Chambers read books, but he saw scarcely any artisans, and many things are to be learnt only in the workshop.' The Encyclopedia would offer to its reader what he would have learnt by watching the artisan at work, while the artisan would be able to learn from the philo‑ sopher the broader aspects of his labours. The great contribution of Diderot to this desirable end is emphasised. M. Diderot

> is the author of the longest and most important part of this Encyclo‑ pedia, the part most desired by the public, and I dare say the most difficult to execute; that is the description of the arts. M. Diderot has based it upon memoranda which have been furnished to him by workers and by amateurs . . . upon the crafts which he has gone to the trouble of observing and for which on occasion he has had models constructed. . . . He has applied himself to this task with a courage worthy of the finest centuries of philosophy. . . .

Moreover, many even of the better articles taken from Chambers required to be rewritten, corrected and abridged. What d'Alembert does not say here is that many articles were taken bodily from Chambers, a practice that was regarded as neither so unusual nor so shocking in that age as it would be today.

Finally, d'Alembert is perfectly frank about the adoption of the alphabetical order. It is more convenient and easy for the reader than any other, and it had been inherited from the old prospectus of 1745[1] 'which was approved by the public and to which we wished to conform'. When Diderot and d'Alembert took the work over many scholars were already 'Well into their work following the original alphabetical project; consequently it would have been impossible for us to change this project, even if we had been less disposed to approve of it.' In short, 'everything combined in obliging us to make this work conform to a plan which we would have followed by choice had we been the masters'. Such frankness was typical of d'Alembert, the orthodox and reputable scholar. When he makes play, as he does, with the scholarly principles and pretensions of the work, we are bound to admit that for his own part he observed the rules to an extent which was not, in fact, true of all the contributors, including Diderot himself on occasion. Likewise, he confesses freely that

[1] Put forth when David Le Breton first made terms with Mills and Sellius for a transla‑ tion of Chambers, ten years before Diderot and d'Alembert took it over.

the great work could not be definitive. He admits its likely inadequacies, for he knows as well as anyone that an Encyclopedia is the work of centuries. The Editors must be satisfied to have laid the foundations. They have dedicated their labours to posterity and the Great Being who never dies. The dedication is framed in capital letters: À LA POSTÉRITÉ ET À L'ÊTRE QUI NE MEURT POINT.

The list of contributors with which the *Discours* concludes affords a valuable idea of the breadth of the sources upon which the Encyclopedia drew at its inception.[1] The subscribers must have been suitably impressed by the prospective quality of a work which promised to draw upon Daubenton, the colleague of Buffon, for its natural history; the Abbé Mallet, Royal Professor of Theology at Paris, for its theology and its articles on history and literature; Dumarsais for grammar; the Abbé Yvon for metaphysics, logic and ethics; while it called upon royal servants like Eidous for heraldry; Le Blond for the military arts in general, not to mention d'Argentville for gardening. The list goes on with the names of men, great and small, physicians to the king, farmers' general, paymasters of the navy, the engineer in charge of the island of Grenada, and Prévost, Inspector of Glassworks, Longchamp the great brewer, Buisson the manufacturer of fabrics at Lyon and La Bassée on lacework. Barrat, 'Excellent worker in his trade, has assembled and disassembled several times in the presence of M. Diderot that admirable machine, the stocking loom', while Bonnet and Laurent, 'silk workers, have set up and worked a velvet frame, etc., and a frame for brocade, while M. Diderot observed'. There is the wood-engraver, the type-founder, the locksmith and the pewterer. There is even an Englishman, 'M. Hill', who has communicated a model of an English glassworks 'executed in relief and all its instruments, with the necessary explanations'. No documents in the history of technology can compare with this inventory of the trades of France in the middle of the eighteenth century. To dip into such resources is like looking at a glass bee-hive, or stumbling upon a busy ant-hill in calm and sunshine.

[1] The extension of its sources is described in Chapter 15.

Chapter Thirteen

THE FIRST SEVEN VOLUMES

IN the autumn of 1751, when the first volume had been out for several months, d'Alembert's *Discours* was reviewed in the *Journal des Scavans*. It was conceded that the author had written eloquently on the spirituality of the soul and the existence of God, even if he was more generally charged with 'an affected laconicism' in respect of religion. The review was a danger-signal in its warning of the dangers of the Lockeian system which d'Alembert took for granted as the orthodoxy. 'The system of Locke is dangerous for religion', he was warned, 'although one has no objections to make when those who adopt it do not draw noxious conclusions from it.'

Among the crowd of abbés recruited for the Encyclopedia were two, M. Mallet and M. Yvon, of whom d'Alembert especially boasted in his list of contributors. In the same house with them there lodged a somewhat saturnine young man with a pock-marked face called the Abbé Jean-Martin de Prades, a bachelor of theology at the Sorbonne who was about to submit his doctrinal dissertation, *Majeure ordinaire*. The Sorbonne examined the thesis, asked the author a number of questions, and proceeded to grant him his doctorate. Not until several months had passed was it realised that the Abbé de Prades had drawn very noxious conclusions from John Locke, and that his thesis was as full of heresy as an egg is full of meat. He had in fact written an essay in defence of Natural Religion.

Rather late in the day the Doctors of the Sorbonne picked out ten propositions which they declared to be 'false, rash, harmful . . . erroneous, blasphemous, materialist, dangerous to society and the public peace', etc., etc. The Abbé's doctorate was revoked, his examiner was dismissed, and the candidate obliged to make off in the direction of Berlin, where Frederick the Great could generally be relied upon to provide a refuge for other people's heretics. It was a most embarrassing business for everyone concerned. The Sorbonne, being an organisation rather than an individual, was unable to blush, but it promptly and unblushingly indulged in a complete *volte-face*. Nevertheless the doctors of the Sorbonne were bound to ask themselves how they had been duped, how they could have entertained heresy unawares, and even awarded a doctorate to a heretic?

They decided, as may be imagined, that the blame lay in the young abbé's cunning rather than in their own sloth. The true answer, however, was wholly creditable to their intellectual integrity, for they had origin- ally examined de Prades's thesis on its intellectual merits and not in accordance with their own organisational necessities, and they had found it wholly convincing. If, on looking at it again as an organisation with an orthodoxy to defend, they decided that it was heretical, all that they had done – and it is done every day – was to make clear once more the dis- tinction between intellectual integrity and institutional necessity. The origin of the abbé's 'errors', as they were now called, stemmed from his original premise: that all human knowledge originates in sensation. The doctors of the Sorbonne knew as well as John Locke that this was incon- trovertibly true. They were all Lockeians *sans peur et sans tache*. Perhaps they believed the Abbé Condillac when he said that he was developing Locke in such a way that the enemies of religion could not make an abuse of him! Anyway, it was only now that they realised where the proposition could lead to. The Abbé de Prades had opened the eyes of the Faculty to 'the poison of Locke'. As another abbé, Loménie de Brienne, put it:

> Nothing is better calculated for making obvious the system that places the origin of our ideas in the impression of the senses than does the use that the enemies of religion make of it. Doubtless because it has been regarded as merely a philosophical opinion there has been no alarm over the favour gained by the system, even in the Schools of the University, during the past few years. But the impious thesis of M. de Prades has finally opened people's eyes concerning the disturbing consequences that result from it.

Long afterwards, believing himself to have detected the same poison at work in England, Coleridge was to write that 'what is bred in the bone . . . will break out in the flesh'. How, he asked in deploring the influence of Mr Locke, is it possible to keep together pious conclusions and atheistic premises? The Lockeian tradition, he thought, led on through Low Church Protestantism at home to the Encyclopedists abroad, and finally to the Jacobins' Goddess of Reason.

The moral of this affecting story is that the Abbé de Prades had con- sorted with the Encyclopedists, indeed was the author of the article on CERTITUDE in volume two, which came out at the height of the uproar over his thesis. Not only did he lodge in the same house as the Abbé Mallet and the Abbé Yvon, the two gentlemen of whom d'Alembert had boasted as scholars of light and leading in his *Discours*, but he was suspected of having served as a stooge for Diderot himself, and there is little doubt that the Encyclopedists encouraged him. When it came to his writing a three-volume apologia from exile, the third volume seems to have been written by Diderot. And when in 1754, after recanting his errors, he proposed to write a work on the truth of religion, it was again Diderot who suggested that he should preface it with a restatement of all his calumnies. It came to nothing. Perhaps he felt that he had done enough for freedom when he sacrificed his doctorate. He fades from view as an archdeacon and the author of a lost translation of Tacitus. In so far as he survives in history at all, it is as a kind of ventriloquist's doll for Diderot and d'Alembert.

It was not really surprising that the attack on the Abbé de Prades led to an attack on the Encyclopedia. The Jesuits in particular were awaiting their opportunity, for they were incensed at not being entrusted with the theological articles, and d'Alembert expected them to mount a full-dress offensive at any moment. The de Prades scandal furnished them with precisely the opportunity they knew best how to make use of, for they were skilled politicians, and the Court was already joining in the fracas. In the New Year, the Bishop of Mirepoix, a pro-Jesuit who was tutor to the Dauphin, went to the King in tears and begged him for an *arrêt de conseil* to suppress the Encyclopedia and prohibit its further publication and distribution. On 7 February, when the second volume was only just out, it was declared that His Majesty has found that in these volumes

a point has been made of inserting several maxims tending to destroy the royal authority, to establish a spirit of independence and revolt, and under cover of obscure and ambiguous terminology to build the foundations of error, of moral corruption and of unbelief.

And as Montauban, the Abbé de Prades's bishop said, if Hell which had hitherto vomited its venom drop by drop was now emitting it in torrents it was all the fault of the *Philosophes*. Impiety was becoming a system.

The Encyclopedists, it was once said, were mistaken in not believing in Providence, for it was obviously for their sake that Providence gave the direction of the book-trade to Malesherbes.[1] In the crises of 1751–2 it was Malesherbes who saved the licence. There were other saviours, too. Madame de Pompadour, arch-enemy of the Jesuits, was one. She used all

---

[1] Lamoignon de Malesherbes was *Directeur de la librairie* from 1750 to 1763, which means that he supervised the publishing trade and controlled licences for printing.

her considerable influence with the King to enable the work to continue. The powers that be, at least the secular powers, were anxious that it should continue in some form. There were powerful considerations that it was difficult to ignore: the vested interests of the large body of sub‑ scribers, respect for their property, the preservation of the printing trade, not to mention the importance of keeping money at home which otherwise threatened to migrate to neighbouring countries, most prob‑ ably to Holland. Resumption was not allowed explicitly by public act or decree; it was permitted on sufferance, under a common form of evasion of that time, a *licence tacite*, which was frequently extended to a publisher in the case of a work the authorities had to tolerate while not wishing to admit it.

When he wrote the preface to the third volume, d'Alembert spoke of the Government's appearing to desire that the enterprise should not be abandoned. Melchior de Grimm, the great literary gossip of the *Philosophe* party, tells us that the government could find no alternative to the existing editors. For all their fuss, the Jesuits had proved incapable of taking over the work. They lacked the 'keys', or the technical know‑ ledge of the organisation, and they certainly had no *tête* to compare with that of Denis Diderot. All the same, the crisis was to have some unfor‑ tunate consequences. While it had a certain publicity‑value, so that the number of subscribers went up from two to three thousand, it left the hitherto indispensable d'Alembert in a position to dispense a certain righteous and martyr‑like tone in the preface to the next volume. 'The eagerness that has been shown for the continuation of this dictionary is the sole motive that could have induced us to take it up again', he said. In other words, as the actress says in emerging from retirement, 'in response to overwhelming public demand. . . .' The martyr came out in such phrases as 'May posterity love us as men of virtue, even if it does not esteem us as men of letters', an expression typical of that yearning for secular immortality which so often afflicts men who are unable to believe in a heaven beyond this world.[1]

New censors had been appointed, largely by Mirepoix, and everyone knew it. It was therefore the more necessary for d'Alembert to assure the subscribers that no 'undertakings' had been entered into and that the Encyclopedia was unchanged as regards its *esprit de Philosophe*. No one, now or in the future, neither prince nor grandee, would be allowed to contribute by virtue of rank or privilege. 'This Encyclopedia owes every‑ thing to talents, nothing to titles, and is the history of the human spirit,

[1] Cf. Diderot in his article ENCYCLOPÉDIE, and p. 6 above.

not of the vanity of men.' And as happens frequently in consequence of a dose of persecution, the work showed a progressive improvement from volume three onwards. New areas of interest began to appear. Economics and political economy, subjects especially interesting to a middle-class public, came in under C, with topics like 'COMMERCE', and 'COMPETI- TION' and 'EXCHANGE'. To deal with this work, Forbonnais was an im- pressive recruit. Turgot, a friend of d'Alembert, who had already con- tributed a memorandum on 'COTTON', was to supply five excellent articles on philosophy and economics. Legal and administrative institu- tions were treated in some informative and dispassionate work by Boucher d'Argis, and the art of healing (under CRISE) was tackled by d'Alembert's medical friend, Bordeu. D'Alembert himself wrote an article on COLLÉGE in which he got his own back on Jesuit educationists. The latest contributors were men of genuine and dispassionate learning who could supply the ballast of real specialisation to a work that was often in danger of succumbing to the temptations of being flighty and super- ficial.

Most important of all was the arrival in volume three of the Chevalier de Jaucourt. A man of ancient family who had received his education at a number of universities, including Geneva, Leyden and Cambridge, he was a Protestant, a Doctor of Medicine, and a member of numerous learned societies. Cosmopolitan and urbane, the Chevalier was also a gentleman of great integrity and of a purity of character somewhat excep- tional among the *Philosophes*, a psychological asset of no mean order. Not an original mind, rather a sissors-and-paste man, he could always be depended upon to turn out promptly the innumerable short articles that an Encyclopedia demands. He was a great aid to Diderot, who somewhat ungraciously used to refer to him as 'The Mill', or the article-grinder. Without Jaucourt it is difficult to imagine how the editorship would have survived successfully through its later and most difficult years.

Volume four turned out to be the most objective and the least contro- versial of all so far. The work had settled down. In 1754 d'Alembert, whose *Mélanges* had come out in 1753, was elected to the Académie Française. This was regarded as something more than a purely personal tribute, indeed as a victory for the Encyclopedia and the 'new philo- sophy'. It certainly increased the confidence and the self-esteem of the Encyclopedic party. And it is at this point that the *Philosophes* begin to bear the unmistakable features of a party, or as was often said at the time, a sect. It is not merely the effect of backbiters like Fréron and Palissot with their scoffing at the *Cacouacs*, and their accusation of mutual 'incense-burning'. There are also many signs of what may be called 'recruitment by success'. The greater the success of the Encyclopedia the more readily eminent men joined forces with the movement, and the more eminent contributors came in the more the success. D'Alembert was able to announce Voltaire as a contributor to volume five. Now that the work had acquired a certain solidity, now that it had become less obviously controversial and more steadily unexceptionable, it was possible to recruit Voltaire to the crew without the danger of sinking the boat. His adherence was regarded as a tremendous catch, for he was the most famous writer in Europe, the writer whom every educated person wanted to read and whose opinions about everything everyone wanted to know. Even so, at first d'Alembert was happier to make use of the great man's name rather than his pen, and kept him as much as possible to the field of literary criticism where his peculiarly 'Voltairean' views could do least to upset the orthodox. The next 'star turn', so to speak, was announced in the preface to volume five, taking the form of an *éloge* of Montesquieu. The great man, of whom d'Alembert had written in sincere praise in the *Discours* (much to his pleasure), had died in 1755. He had always been reluctant to contribute, and it is sad that we were not to be given the requested articles by him on 'DEMOCRACY' and 'DESPOTISM'. When he died his sole contribution was an unfinished article on 'TASTE'. In his *éloge* in volume five d'Alembert declared: 'We consider one of the most honourable rewards for our labour to be the particular interest which M. de Montesquieu took in this Dictionary.' He proposed to give the fragmentary essay he had left behind to the world exactly as it stood, and would 'treat it with the same respect antiquity formerly showed to the last words of Seneca'. When he added that only his death had prevented Montesquieu from extending further his kindnesses towards the Encyclopedists he was, of course, giving utterance to a pleasing half-truth. Montesquieu had held himself apart from the Encyclopedists out of profound differences of temper and outlook. He shared their animosities but scarcely their enthusiasms. This did not discourage them in their favourite editorial game of 'name-dropping', which is a modest term for what the Encyclopedists were prepared to indulge in.

The later 1750s were not a favourable time for the dissemination of new ideas. France was losing the Seven Years War and busy looking for scapegoats. In times of national disaster and lost battles a despotic government has a familiar habit of making propitiatory sacrifices to the national deities. When Frederick of Prussia thrashed the pride of the

French army at Rossbach and the English were winning on sea and land (Quiberon Bay and Minden in 1759) not to speak of the victories of Clive and Wolfe in distant continents, east and west, and when in the midst of these reverses a crazy young man tried to assassinate Louis the Well-Beloved with a penknife, it was thought high time to make a few examples. The publication of Helvétius's 'poisonous' book, *De l'esprit*, in the summer of 1758 brought the spirit of vengefulness to a head. Though Helvétius was not a contributor to the Encyclopedia, his work was easily equated in people's minds, especially those of the reviewers, with the Encyclopedia, and by the end of the year (the first in which no volume had appeared) the storm was beginning to blow.

Chapter Fourteen

THE CRISIS

THE attack on the Encyclopedia in 1759 differed somewhat from that of 1751–2. The earlier attack had come from the King's Council. Largely as a result of the tactical skill of Malesherbes, it is thought, this had forestalled the Parlement of Paris. In the second attack it was the Parlement that took the offensive through Omer Joly de Fleury, the Attorney-General. He spoke of 'a project formed, a society organised, to propagate materialism, to destroy religion, to inspire a spirit of independence, and to nourish the corruption of morals'. In fact, the Attorney-General adopted the favourite myth of satirists: that the Encyclopedists were a sect aiming at the overturn of church and state. He mentioned especially the wicked works of Diderot, of which the Encyclopedia was declared to be an 'abridgement'. The technique of the *renvoi*, the cross-reference, of which Diderot had spoken openly and with pride, was now blamed for much of the evil. 'All the venom of this Dictionary is to be found in the cross-references.' By a decree in February the Parlement ordered the suspension of the sale and distribution of the work pending the examination of the volumes already out. For this task a committee of nine Jansenists, three of them Doctors of Divinity, was set up. The decree recited the offensive doctrines promulgated in the first seven volumes, which was an unfortunate tactic, for it was duly noted that more people were likely to read the few pages of this recitation than would ever read the seven volumes. This time, the Parlement had forestalled the Monarchy, and the Encyclopedia was a pawn in the contest of the two. On 8 March the King stepped in and on the Chancellor Lamoignon de Malesherbes's advice ordered the suppression of the Encyclopedia *in toto*. The licence was revoked.

Could the national advantages to be derived from the great work with regard to the arts and sciences compensate for the damage it was doing to morality and religion? This time it seemed that even economic considerations and the property rights of subscribers were to be brushed aside in a great national act of propitiation. The capital at stake however

was very large. The subscribers now numbered some 4,000, they had
paid far more cash than they had received value for in seven volumes,
while 4,000 copies of the eighth volume were actually ready for distribution. If the publishers were to be required to make good the loss without
being able to make further profits they would go bankrupt. It was hard
to believe that so important a section of the trade of Paris would be
allowed to suffer ruin. Despite all the fulminations of authority there yet
seems to have been a widespread belief that the trade would somehow be
able to complete the enterprise.

On an evening at the end of April, the editors, along with the Baron
d'Holbach, dined with Le Breton, the chief of the publishers. As La
Mettrie had said, 'what a power there is in a repast!' The evening ended
with d'Alembert declaring that he would no longer co-operate, except
for the correction of the proofs of mathematical articles. He had been
bowing himself out for some time past, and he was to keep his word.
Diderot, however, ended the session swearing that he would see the work
to its conclusion despite hell and high water. He was always at his best
in a fight. Voltaire, of course, suggested taking the work to Prussia, but
Diderot seems to have talked of Holland. Neither was resorted to. No
one really wanted the Encyclopedia to leave France. Public respect for
invested capital was immense. Publication of the successive volumes had
become an annual national event, and people were thirsting for the
promised books. It is notable that not a single subscriber asked for his
money back throughout the crisis, although the royal decree entitled
each to a refund of 72 livres, which represented the difference between
the sum paid and the value of the volumes already published. This fact
was probably the decisive point, proving as nothing else could the confidence and goodwill of the public. From the summer of 1759 for nearly
six years Diderot, with the Chevalier de Jaucourt, slaved behind locked
doors. Everyone knew what was going on. It was an open secret. Malesherbes, the old ally, excelled himself. When Diderot's personal safety was
threatened as a result of tale-telling, Malesherbes gave him advance
information of the intended search and arrest. He urged Diderot to
make his escape from Paris or to go into hiding. And in reply to Diderot's
objection that he could hardly transport his papers on such a flight,
Malesherbes simply offered his own house as a safe hiding-place for them.
No one, he said, would think of looking there. It was the kind of episode
that relieves what Thomas Carlyle called 'the wicked old eighteenth century' of much of its blameworthiness in the memory of men of good will.
It helps to make the work of the eighteenth-century scholar a labour of love.

The last ten volumes were all published together in 1765–6, and eleven volumes of plates between 1762 and 1772. Everyone knew that the place of publication on the title,page, 'Neuchâtel', meant Paris, but nobody said so, which is simply another instance of that looking,glass world which was the old France. But the most absurd feature was the censorship. It is obvious that the proscribed work could not have been submitted to censors, let alone be passed by them, yet censored this work was – by the printers. The absence of official censorship meant that the volumes were sure to contain some pretty risky criticisms concerning both Church and State. The proof,readers were bound, even if only from self,interest, to read everything with special care. The original frankness of the editors – more especially in the matter of the *renvois* – had taught everyone where to look for dangerous matter. Now the printers, compositors and proof, readers were themselves to do the job of the censors, secular and ec, clesiastical, and to do it better. Le Breton, the King's Printer, and his chief compositor, secretly went over everything with the blackest of black ink. When Diderot discovered what they had done he wrote to Le Breton in typically Dideronian style:

> You have driven a dagger into my heart . . . For two years you have deceived me like a coward. You have massacred like a brutish beast the work of twenty honest men . . . an atrocity of which there is no example in the history of books . . . I wept with rage . . . You have made our work flat and insipid . . .

It went on for pages.

We know now the extent of the injury. In 1947 two American scholars published *The Censoring of Diderot's Encyclopedia*, based on the discovery of an extra volume containing the greater part of the censored material, decorated with large black crosses.[1] The heaviest cuts are in Diderot's own articles on 'Pyrrhonism' and 'Saracens'.[2] Some shorter articles on Protestantism and the Christian sects are wholly struck out. The wicked work was skilfully done, and Diderot greatly overstated the injury. It is true that he was the chief victim, and after him the Chevalier de Jau, court. One complete article by Morellet was removed bodily. The re, mainder was largely respected. There was no cause for a general outcry

---

[1] The 318 pages of proof from various volumes of the Encyclopedia had passed from Le Breton to the Fonds Vandeul in Leningrad whence it returned to France, being bought by a Baltimore bibliophile, D. H. Gordan. Such is the basis of the work by D. H. Gordan and N. L. Torrey (New York, 1947).

[2] Containing the typical remark, 'religion declines as philosophy grows . . . the more philosophers there are in Constantinople, the fewer pilgrims there will be to Mecca'.

and none came, although Diderot kept up a long complaint that the subscribers 'have subscribed for my work and it is almost yours that you are giving them'. When all is said and done, the King's Printer could have been expected neither to play fast and loose with the sacred institutions of Church and State nor risk the confiscation and official condemnation of the final volumes and the consequent loss of the enormous private capital invested in them. Even so, Le Breton was to suffer a week in the Bastille for having released copies to the Court at their own request! Diderot can hardly have resisted a certain satisfaction at this. His chief feeling, however, was one of relief at the conclusion of his task. 'I shall scarcely go there any more', he wrote in July, 'to that damned shop where I wore out my eyes . . . The burden I have carried for twenty years has bent me so well that I despair of ever straightening up again.' In August he is reckoning on another week's labour, 'after which I shall cry: Land! Land!' Le Breton's financial arrangements proved generous, so that he rejoiced again: 'All my debts will be paid off, and I shall walk on the earth as light as a feather.'

The twenty years of dangerous toil were over, and the world had the Encyclopedia. When we recall the character of the men who made it, and more especially their chief, it is scarcely possible to imagine the venture having failed. It remains 'the true centre of a history of ideas in the eight-eenth century'.

Le Breton's activities could not, and did not, destroy its scientific and critical spirit. Perhaps the principal damage suffered was not in conse-quence of the work of Le Breton but of the fact that the final volumes had to be finished 'in darkness'. The year-by-year publication had been valuable. For some eight years it had been possible to check each volume as it came out. As Grimm said in a letter he wrote on New Year's Day in 1771, it was valuable to see the effects of each volume as it appeared, making up for defects as they were revealed. The unloading of ten vol-umes in little more than twelve months was bound to mean that some-thing was lost.

Chapter Fifteen

THE OPEN CONSPIRACY

'A project formed, a society organised . . .' Perhaps it was in such accusations of conspiracy that the thesis originated which proposed, as Coleridge once put it, 'to solve the riddle of the French Revolution by anecdotes', or which made it the work of the Freemasons, the Rosicrucians, the Illuminati to which Mozart belonged. Looking back in 1790 Edmund Burke spoke of 'a literary cabal' which had some years ago 'formed a regular plan for the destruction of the Christian religion'. Burke had been in France only once and that was in 1772, when he had been profoundly shocked by what he called 'this conspiracy of atheism'. Nothing was wanting to this faction but 'the power of carrying the intolerance of the tongue and the pen into a persecution which would strike at property, liberty, and life'. Burke's language is almost a paraphrase of that used by Omer Joly de Fleury, the Attorney-General in 1759. It was to be his language for years to come, developing the conspiratorial theory of the origins of the Revolution until it became the upthrust of the Satanic element, very much in anticipation of Joseph de Maistre himself. 'From the tomb of this murdered monarchy', he was to write, 'has emerged an immense and formless monster, more terrible than any that has hitherto stunned and subjugated the imagination of mankind.' This strange and hideous monster apparently went straight for its prey without fear or remorse. It was to be seen rehearsing the uncoiling of its fearful length in the years of the *Philosophes* and the Encyclopedists.

How much truth is there behind this theory of conspiracy? There existed, said Madame de Genlis, 'A conspiracy bound by solemn oaths and holding secret meetings . . . a veritable army of conspirators . . . a sect obedient to the same watchword . . .' This implied organisation, this conspiratorial discipline with its single command, are nonsense. Even if it is intended to attribute these characteristics to the men who wrote the Encyclopedia it would refer only to some 130 persons, among whom the leading characters amounted to about twenty. Grimm was right when he said that most of them did not even know one another by sight. As for the secrecy, the 'conspiracy' if it existed was an open one, conducted for long enough under royal licence; for the work to be done could not have been carried on without such patronage. It was a conspiracy which em, bodied the intelligentsia of France, no less.

A plot generally involves a sinister objective. In this case, according to its enemies, a plot to undermine the very foundations of the social order itself. And a plot for so extensive and malign a purpose must evince a certain unity of doctrine. René Hubert, after examining the seventeen volumes of the Encyclopedia, concluded that contemporaries were right when they thought of it as 'a great and, as it were, anonymous work'. 'Throughout all its variations', he claimed to discover 'a positive funda, mental doctrine'. It was, of course, part of the essential nature of a work intended to display 'the connecting together of the branches of human knowledge in a methodical, coherent and systematic order'. After all, this was far from being concealed by the editors. Rather it was declared, even boasted, by both d'Alembert in his *Discours préliminaire* and by Diderot in the article ENCYCLOPÉDIE, as we have seen: 'The end of an encyclopedia is to bring together the branches of knowledge, thereby revealing the general system to which they belong.' A mere dictionary of definitions and details would not have been an encyclopedia, or a circle of knowledge, but a compendium. 'This,' Diderot reminded his subscribers, 'signifies *enchaînement des connaissances.*'

Who, after all, were the men who wrote the work? *'Une société de gens de lettres'* said the title,page, thereby admitting, even proclaiming, the notion of a collective. It was inaugurated by a comparatively obscure writer whose ideas at the beginning were still unsettled, unresolved; and by a mathematician of genius whose position on general questions was first revealed in the preliminary discourse. The twin chiefs actually ar, rived at their settled views in the course of editing the work, perhaps even as they read the views of their contributors. As for these last, they were first of all a number of Diderot's allied translators: Toussaint, Eidous, Deleyre, Desmahis. Then came superior journalists, *belle, lettristes, folliculaires*, occasionally a prize,essayist like Rousseau, many writers of little works in the form of the *discours, essai* and *entretiens*, all of which were favourite literary forms of the extremely vocal society to which the *Philosophes* belonged. Among such writers we find Marmontel, Saint,Lambert, Boulanger, Naigeon, and later Morellet. Such, then, was the original nucleus of the *société de gens de lettres*. To them were recruited, principally by d'Alembert, the *savants*, and the *érudits*, a pro, cess which represents the rallying of learning to letters, ensuring that the work would not be that of a faction. D'Alembert brought in members of the Academies of Paris and of Montpellier. Specialists like the distinguished philologist, the Abbé Sallier, Professor of Hebrew of the Collège de France, a member of the Académié des Inscriptions and the Académie de France, Keeper of the King's Library. The Abbé Sallier was a great asset for research purposes, as d'Alembert recorded gratefully in the *Discours*. In Boucher d'Argis, who appeared in volume three, was secured a member of an ancient family of *parlementaires*, of liberal education and temperament, who combined reformist notions with respect for the traditional institutions of France. The same can be said of historians like Lenglet Dufresnoy, grammarians like Dumarsais ('whose name alone is sufficient recommendation'), and geographers like d'Anville and Bellin. From the pens of such men the subscribers could feel assured that they were getting news as well as views, and news of sound quality. Such savants raised the quality of the work from that of a commercial and literary venture to a great academic enterprise. Success itself had a snowball effect with the adhesion of Voltaire, the pillaging of the works of Buffon and Montesquieu, along with a good deal of name-dropping. The work could hardly depart further from that of a sect than when it recruited the assistance of Charles Pinot Duclos, the confirmed enemy of the sectarianism, indeed the fanaticism, of the *Philosophes*. Nor must be forgotten the value of the work done by 'the common man', if the time and the place will permit such a term, the occasional writer, the amateur, the man whose special knowledge of some special field made him a valuable instructor of the 'common man' who would read his work. This group includes not only businessmen and technicians, manufacturers and master-craftsmen, but even the Keeper of the Royal Hunting Preserves who wrote the article CERF. Finally there was the fringe of abbés, working downwards from Mallet and de Prades.

The best guarantee that the Encyclopedia was a great deal more, and other, than a revolutionary work is provided by the lists of subscribers. It was bought by the people to whom it was addressed, the enlightened bourgeoisie. It could not have been afforded by any lower social strata. The *bourgeoisie moyenne* is the best description of its public. The character of these people was Gallican, liberal and monarchist. They were not in the least a 'revolutionary class' but men who hoped for reform without envisioning the possibility, or the desirability, of radical changes in the national constitution or in traditional French *mœurs*, men who were conscious of their own wealth and intelligence and resentful at their exclusion from the management of affairs, the men whose social order was to come to power in the great revolution. The Encyclopedists themselves were largely men of this class and were con-sciously writing for it. That they should have been deliberately planning to undermine the foundations of France's political and social institutions would have been, as René Hubert said, 'the most absurd of contradic-tions'.

An aspect of the Encyclopedia that has been too little appreciated in later times is its wit, its satire, its sheer comedy. Much of this stems from the rather poker-faced humour of Pierre Bayle. It springs straight from the soil which bred Montaigne and Rabelais. There are even elements of self-mockery that remind us of Flaubert's *Bouvard et Pécuchet*. In the twentieth century it is necessary to imagine a composite work produced under an editorial board consisting of H. G. Wells, Bernard Shaw, Bertrand Russell and Julian Huxley, with Lytton Strachey as Voltaire, and all the liberal intelligentsia from Gilbert Murray to Leonard Woolf ready to send in their essays.

PART IV
The Philosophes and the Revolution

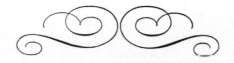

Chapter Sixteen

THE POLITICS OF THE
PHILOSOPHES

T̶h̶e̶ ̶Philosophes ̶c̶o̶n̶t̶r̶i̶b̶u̶t̶e̶d̶ ̶l̶i̶t̶t̶l̶e̶ ̶t̶o̶ ̶p̶o̶l̶i̶t̶i̶c̶a̶l̶ ̶t̶h̶o̶u̶g̶h̶t̶,̶ ̶i̶n̶v̶e̶n̶t̶i̶n̶g̶ ̶n̶o̶t̶h̶i̶n̶g̶
new or original. Originality was not called for. Every feasible political
idea, and some lacking in feasibility, was already at home in the world.
What was wanted now was practice, the bringing into operation of the
ideas and practices of politically civilised people, which means some
form of effective self,government, of liberty under law, or guarantee for
civic and civil rights. The French were shortly to promulgate men's
rights in the form of the Declaration of the Rights of Man. When they
did so their English,speaking neighbours and transatlantic allies were not
greatly impressed, for they saw in such statements little more than a
rather rhetorical generalising of their own rights at Common Law. The
Philosophes, like the leaders of the Revolution, talked a great deal about
these rights, but unlike the revolutionaries, they were not called upon to
put them into action. One of the most typical characteristics of the
Philosophes was their confinement to talk and their exclusion from politi,
cal power. Turgot is the only exception, and he, Controller,General for
some two years, found little or no support among his colleagues, and all
the reformist work of his ministry was quickly undone. Despite the
inefficacy of his measures, it remains remarkable that Louis XVI ever
had a *Philosophe* for a minister.

In so far as the *Philosophes* taught any properly political ideas they
were mostly the ideas of a kind of academic Whiggery. Limited mon,
archy, the separation of powers, the rule of law, the politics of liberty, all
are to be found in the teachings of Montesquieu and some in those of
Voltaire, both of whom were something more and in most respects
something other than *Philosophes*. A typical *Philosophe* like d'Holbach
recited the political theories of John Locke as if they were the beginning
and the end of wisdom, and the political articles of the Encyclopedia,
some of which he wrote, were for the most part of the self,same inspira,

E

tion. An Englishman could, and did, approve of the politics of the
Encyclopedia in very English terms. 'Whoever takes the trouble of
combining the several political articles', wrote an English reviewer in the
1760s, 'will find that they form a noble system of civil liberty.' Burke was
fond of professing his attachment to what he called a 'manly liberty',
and it is pleasing to discover at least one thing in which the Encyclopedists
resembled Burke. But then they both stemmed from a common parent
in Locke.

The reformism of the *Philosophes* might lead one to imagine that the
Revolution was the harvest of what they had sown. It was in fact rather
an arrest upon it, for reformism is often the enemy of revolution. The
effect of the French Revolution upon the reformism of eighteenth-
century France was like the effect of the Reformation upon the Renaissance. It brought reaction in an age of increasing liberalism: reaction
in the direction of an intolerant and persecuting ideology, for it was, as
de Tocqueville was the first to point out, a political movement that bore
most of the features of a religious movement. Hopes of peaceful change
and moderate reform were quickly dashed, and the *ancien régime* went
up in flames. The new world, men said, must be built by burning the
records of the old. The old order was to be drowned in blood, ravaged
by war. Those who carried through the process became increasingly
convinced that it deserved its fate. 'These outrages', Tom Paine was to
say, 'were not the effect of the principles of the Revolution but of the
degraded mind that existed before the Revolution and which the Revolution is calculated to reform.'

All the leading *Philosophes* were dead by the time of the Revolution.
There was indeed a great mortality in their ranks during the ten years
before the fall of the Bastille. Condillac died in 1780, d'Alembert in 1783,
Diderot in 1784, Buffon in 1788, d'Holbach in 1789. It was as if the celestial scene-shifter of the stage of history mercifully decided to shift not
only the old scenery but the old actors. Condorcet, who lingered on until
1794, died in his cell before he could be guillotined.[1] It is of course impossible to say what any of the others would have done if they had lived
into the revolutionary years, although it is to be imagined that like
Condorcet they would have been Girondins rather than Jacobins, for
they were not revolutionary types, and if they possessed anything so
singular as a creed it was not a revolutionary one. If they had anything
political to say aside from their Whig orthodoxy, it was to express their
hopes of reformist initiative at the hands of some enlightened prince or

---

[1] Probably he poisoned himself.

'instructed minority'. Helvétius quoted with approval the maxim of Frederick the Great: 'Nothing is better than arbitrary rule by just, humane and virtuous princes.' On the whole, however, he put his faith in an enlightened minority, a utilitarian *étatisme*. For, as Condillac said, 'the light dawns on a privileged few and always illuminates a limited horizon'. The enlightened few have the privilege, indeed the duty, of leading along the rest, *compelling* them towards the light if they are reluctant. The *Philosophes* must often have fancied themselves in the role of Plato's guardians whose task it was to turn the dwellers in the cave towards the light, or as Rousseau expresses it, forcing the rest to be free. No wonder that Coleridge apprehended a certain tendency to despotism among the enlightened, 'a natural affinity between despotism and modern philosophy, notwithstanding the proud pretensions of the latter as the emancipators of the human race'.

The *Philosophes* show a certain moral indifference to the means by which their enlightened ends were to be achieved. It is, perhaps, hardly surprising that, like their enemies the Jesuits, they tended to put their faith rather in those who actually possessed the *power* to put their ideas into effect, in other words to entrust the cause of the people to despots. The English *Philosophe*, Jeremy Bentham, spoke in the early days of his long career of the absurdity of 'transporting power into the hands of those whom an invincible ignorance will not permit to use it except for their own destruction'. With few exceptions, the *Philosophes* reserved their admiration for princes like Frederick II of Prussia and Catherine II of Russia. The great exception here was Diderot who always shunned the Court of Frederick the Great and lectured Catherine until she felt bound to tell him that his 'fine ideas' made fine books but 'bad business'. He could write on paper, she said, but she had to write on the human skin, which was 'devilish irritable'. Diderot knew that what people do for themselves is better than what a despot, however enlightened, did for them. Short-cuts to human betterment are attractive, but the long way round which is involved in democracy is to be preferred in the end. 'Arbitrary rule by a just and enlightened prince is always bad', he said. Two enlightened despots in succession could sap a people's devotion to liberty and fatally undermine their initiative. If the great English despot, Elizabeth I, had been followed by a second, even the English would have fallen into slavery.

If the *Philosophes* contributed little that was new or original to political ideas, they may be said to have done something better. They brought to bear upon politics a new attitude to the world of which politics and government are a part. This, and not a specific type of political doctrine, is their contribution to the politics of the modern world. John Morley put it thus:

> The Encyclopedia was virtually a protest against the old organization, no less than against the old doctrine. Broadly stated, the great central moral of it all was this: that human nature is good, that the world is capable of being made a desirable abiding-place, and that the evil of the world is the fruit of bad education and bad institutions.

This cheerful doctrine, he thought, writing in 1878, now struck on the ear as a commonplace, but a century earlier it was the beginning of a new dispensation, and every social improvement since has been the outcome of that doctrine in one form or another. The *Philosophes* were far less interested in political organisation than in society. They concerned themselves less in politics than in manners and morals, the scientific study of *les mœurs*, the subject that is now called sociology. Voltaire, in his great *Essai sur les mœurs* (1740–56), set the example by substituting social for political history. He was writing it for Madame du Châtelet, who was weary of the story of kings, and in his *Avant-propos* he said: 'It is not the purpose of this work to tell the reader in what year a prince unworthy of being remembered succeeded to the government of a barbarous prince over an uncultivated people.' He would omit 'the common kings', or the dead wood of history, and present Madame with a history worthy of her mind, a history of '*l'esprit, les mœurs, les usages*'. He had written in a letter of 1735 that a canal-sluice, a picture by Poussin, a fine tragedy, a truth established, are all of them things a thousand times more precious than the whole mass of annals of the court and all the narratives of campaigns. From the way he wrote his *Essai* he earned the right to be remembered as the father of social history.

Here is the germ of the superabundant attention which the Encyclopedia devoted to the arts and sciences. Here also, if anywhere, are to be found the class-affiliations of the *Philosophes* who wrote it, even (if we must use the term) their contribution to the growth of democracy.

> Contempt for the mechanical arts [wrote d'Alembert in the *Discours préliminaire*] seems to have affected even their inventors. The names of these benefactors of mankind are almost unknown, whereas the destroyers of the race – that is to say, the conquerors – are known to everyone. Yet it is perhaps among the artisans that we must look for sagacity, patience, and resourcefulness.

As for the ploughman, the *laboureur*, the Encyclopedia speaks up for him with all the fervour of the Physiocrats, allies of the *Philosophes*, with their economic doctrine that the land was the source of all wealth, and that consequently the farmers, great and small, were the most valuable element of society. *Le laboureur*, begins the article of that name, is not the drudge who grooms horses and tends beasts and drives the plough. We are ignorant of his proper estate if we think of it in terms of grossness, indigence and contempt. If he is poor, so much the worse for the country, which in that case must itself suffer poverty. 'Thus the degree of well, being of the labourer is perhaps the most precise thermometer of the well, being of the nation.' The eyes of the government should always be on this 'interesting class of men'.

The Chevalier de Jaucourt, who wrote many of the short articles on such topics, turned his attention to the general topic of the PEUPLE. He seems to have based himself mainly upon a *Dissertation sur la nature du peuple* published by the Abbé Coyer at The Hague in 1755. The Abbé's discussion of his subject was heavily ironical, especially as regards the changed meaning of the term in modern times. The Chevalier, however, took it all *au grand sérieux*. The people, we learn, were formerly regarded as the most useful and therefore the most 'respectable' part of the nation. Indeed they *were* the nation, 'the state of the nation in general, as simply opposed to that of the great and noble ranks'. *Le peuple* included not only the ploughmen and the artisans but the merchants, the financiers, the *gens de lettres* and the *gens de loi*. These latter categories, however, have become distinct from the *peuple*. 'The men of law are recruited from a class of the people which attains noble rank without having recourse to the sword; the men of letters, from the instance of Horace, have regarded the people as of little worth', while it has become no longer proper to include in the *peuple* those who practise the fine arts and the luxury trades. The merchants have acquired 'nobility through commerce', and the financiers 'find themselves cheek, by, jowl with the great ones of the realm'. Living luxuriously as they now do, 'it would be absurd to confuse them with the people'. The result is that 'there remain in the mass of the nation only workmen and labourers', people who live in cottages and get up and go to bed by the sun. They are the people who dig the mines and drain the marshes, clean the streets and build our houses. The *laboureurs* are even more bondmen to the courses of nature than the artisans. They are the peasants who till the soil and suffer all the afflictions of nature, not to mention the rich man's con, tumely, the brigandage of the tax, collector, and the ravages of the wild creatures preserved for the pleasures of the powerful. 'Such is the por, trait of the men who make up what we call "the people", and who today

form the most numerous and the most essential part of the nation.' We
have the impudence to imagine that such men have no claim to comfort
unless they remain hard-working and obedient. Why do we expect them
to work hard if their produce is to be swallowed up in taxes and impositions? They especially deserve the protection of the prince, since they
are always the most loyal subjects. Henri IV knew this and was most
careful for their well-being.

As is to be expected the article on PRIVILÈGE contains a measured
condemnation of the injustice suffered by the inferior orders in the
matter of financial exactions. Not only is 'the poorest section of society . . .
always burdened beyond its strength', but 'this section is the most useful
to the state since it consists of those who till the soil and produce the
sustenance of the higher orders'. In the article on REPRÉSENTANTS an
equally measured argument is made for the equitable representation of
all classes. 'As all contribute according to their means to the maintenance
of the commonwealth, so all should be heard.' The familiar words of
Edward I about the approval of all being required for measures affecting
all are paraphrased, and the health and happiness of the sovereign is
identified with a representative system in which there is a just equilibrium
between the citizens of all classes 'which prevents each one of them
sinning against the rest'. There is, however, more than one warning in
this article against what, in the French Revolution, was to be called 'the
never-ending audacity of elected persons'. Although the example of
England is, as usual, cited it is noticeable that the author (probably
d'Holbach) allows his enthusiasm for the English practice of parliamen-
tary institutions to be qualified with a pretty straightforward reference
to the corrupt conduct of the Members of Parliament *vis-à-vis* their
constituents. 'Experience teaches us that countries which flatter themselves the most on their liberties are often those where the people's
representatives betray their interests most frequently, handing over their
constituents to the greed of those who would despoil them.' On the other
hand, the Chevalier de Jaucourt's articles tend to hold up the example
of England with little or no qualification. 'There is one people in the
world which has POLITICAL LIBERTY for the direct objective of its constitution,' he declares in the short articles he devoted to that theme. He will
not claim to decide whether or not the English actually enjoy that bless-
ing, but he is content to cite Montesquieu that 'it is established by their
laws'. Political liberty is founded upon fundamental law which maintains
the separation of powers, and upon 'good civil and constitutional law'
guaranteeing the peace and security of the subject. The limited monarchy

of England is based on the separation and the balance of powers, and it has produced over the centuries 'to the amazement of the world, an equal mixture of liberty and royalty'.

Anyone seeking revolutionary political doctrine in the articles of the Encyclopedia is likely to be disappointed. The men who wrote them, more especially the Chevalier de Jaucourt, were not teachers of the Jacobins. They were rather the pupils of Montesquieu and John Locke. They did not preach liberty, equality and fraternity. They stated clearly and patiently the superiority of limited monarchy, government by con‑ sent, and equitable taxation; the superiority of these things from the point of view of efficiency and prosperity A great deal of the dissatisfac‑ tion which produced the French Revolution was dissatisfaction with the inadequacy of France's ancient institutions to the needs of a modern state, with waste and ineptitude, as well as with justice. The French were finding the old order shameful to the *amour‑propre* of a proud and intelligent people, an indignity to the mind as much as an insult to the feelings, an anachronism rather than an outrage. 'The mildest govern‑ ment of any considerable country in Europe', Arthur Young called it in 1787. It was no iron tyranny requiring to be overthrown by violence, but an antiquated and incompetent despotism requiring the application of common sense. When de Jaucourt wrote his article on the freedom of the press, he did not argue about human rights or intellectual freedom. He simply argued that it was useful: 'The drawbacks of this liberty are so inconsiderable, compared with its advantages, that it ought to be the common law of the whole universe and established under all govern‑ ments.'

When the deputies of the Tiers État went to the Estates‑General in 1789, the common feature in their *cahiers* was the demand that France be given a constitution. From the political articles of the Encyclopedia, with their quotations from Montesquieu and Locke, it is easy to make out what that constitution should be. It was framed in the happy days of the Constitutional Assembly, before bankruptcy and war brought the Jacobins and the Terror.

Chapter Seventeen

HELVÉTIUS

THE elderly gentleman who had led out the dance with little Élisabeth Helvétius was the first *Philosophe*. He died in his hundredth year in January 1757, and Élisabeth's father, Claude-Adrien Helvétius, brought out his famous – or, as many thought, infamous – book in July of the following year. Helvétius was among the last of the *Philosophes* before the Revolution, and *De l'esprit* was among the most scandalous of their works. Claude-Adrien was the third of a line of physicians bearing the latinised version of the name of 'Sweitzer' or 'Swiss' who had once lived at Basle, coming to France via the Palatinate as refugees in 1649. The family fortunes were made out of the Brazilian drug ipecacuana, and the founder was remembered as 'Grand-père Ipécac'. He had cured the Dauphin and earned *lettres de noblesse*. His son performed services for the health of Louis XV and became physician to the Queen, Marie Leczinska. On top of the lucrative family monopoly of ipecacuana, he built up a great fortune by marrying into a family of state-financiers, so that Claude-Adrien, who was born in 1715, was known as 'the spoilt child of finance and fashion'. When the publisher Durand published *De l'esprit* in 1758, it was printed by Moreau, Printer to the Queen and the Dauphin, and it bore the insignia *'avec approbation et privilège du roi'*, although it did not bear the author's name. Everybody knew it was by Claude-Adrien Helvétius, for he had been writing it 'in public' since the middle of the century.

He was obsessed with a passion for literary fame, and had retired from his post as *fermier général* (worth 360,000 livres a year) in order to devote himself to his *chef-d'œuvre* down at his country house at Voré (Orne), spending his winters at his town house in the Rue Sainte-Anne, Paris, where he talked about his work continually at social gatherings. He had been inspired by the success of Montesquieu's *Lettres persanes*. Sometime in the 1740s the older man asked his opinion of the manuscript of an exhaustive study of law and politics, to which he had responded with the advice that before writing a work on the spirit of the laws it was necessary to make an exhaustive study of the mind. Despite Helvétius's advice Montesquieu proceeded to publish his work on the environmental differences between men, while Helvétius applied himself to a similar work on their universal similarities. He would, so to speak, treat the theme of Montesquieu in reverse. In addition to his friendship with the Baron de la Brède et de Montesquieu, his travels about France as *fermier général* had brought him the acquaintance of Comte de Buffon and of the republican champion of toleration and education, Dumarsais, author of the article on 'EDUCATION' for the Encyclopedia. It was Dumarsais who brought home to him the social aspects of education which figure so prominently in *De l'esprit*. A work thus conceived and bearing the *imprimatur* implied in the terms *avec approbation et privilège du roi*', might have been supposed to enjoy the security of orthodoxy. Instead it raised a storm which swept its author from his sinecure office (he was described as Maître d'Hôtel to the Queen) and into exile, first on his estate at Voré, then – though voluntarily – in Germany and England, while his book was burned by the public hangman.

What had he done? Madame du Deffand said that he had given away everyone's secret, the open secret that everyone acts primarily from self-interest. Was this such a shocking revelation? It was the rather dull truism of English philosophic writers like Bernard Mandeville and Alexander Pope, and was developed into the doctrine of enlightened self-interest by Adam Smith and Jeremy Bentham. Mandeville's *Fable of the Bees* bore the slogan 'Private Vices, Public Benefits'. When a benevolent bee founded a colony on principles of virtue the society was ruined, so that the swarm was much concerned to return to the bad old habits which by some alchemy produced the common good. Pope put the idea in the polished couplet in his *Essay on Man*:

> Thus God and Nature fixed the general frame,
> And bade self-love and social be the same.

One might ask could anything be more jejune? Supposing it was true, or true enough, what harm was there in saying so? Helvétius got into trouble not for simply saying so, but for saying it with a great deal of flippancy, paradox and *libertin* anecdotage, and for saying it in the wrong place. His book, propounding these truths, came out on the day when Louisburg ('the strongest fortress in the world') fell to the English, a step on the way to the loss of Canada, or New France. Damiens had already made his attack on the life of Louis XV. Twenty-thousand soldiers of Frederick the Great had defeated sixty-thousand French at

E 2

Rossbach. The Seven Years War was going badly for France, and people were asking whether any better fortunes were to be expected for a people whose moral fibre was being rotted by a gospel of universal self-interest? Helvétius's statement of the gospel was shocking to both the realist and the hypocrite.

His friends had implored Helvétius to publish his book abroad, preferably in Holland. Intent on publishing his masterpiece in the capital city of France he quickly found himself face to face with the consequences of his untimely action. Within a few weeks *De l'esprit* was denounced by the Parlement of Paris and its *privilège* was revoked by the Conseil d'État. The Pope himself declared the book scandalous, licentious and dangerous. The Sorbonne condemned its style and described its contents as containing 'the essence of poison'. Tercier, the censor who had passed the book, was dismissed with a golden handshake of 3,000 livres. Helvétius lost his post as Maitre d'Hôtel to the Queen. He panicked, and made retraction after retraction. Retiring to Voré for two years of exile, he moved heaven and earth to retrieve his position. The Minister, Choiseul, was kinsman to his wife, and Madame de Pompadour was the friend and patron of enlightenment. Both proved cold. The *Philosophes* in general failed to rally round. The notion that they were a united body, standing together through thick and thin, was never more patently disproved. Turgot described the work as 'without logic, without taste and without morality', a case of mistaken violence against a bad but not ill-intentioned government, a maladroit move which bade fair to spoil the prospects of peaceful, ameliorist reform. Diderot was aggrieved in much the same way. Helvétius was not a contributor to the Encyclopedia, but his work was confounded with the great enterprise, and the opportunity to attack it was seized upon as part and parcel of the campaign of 1758 which drove Diderot's labours underground. Even Helvétius's supposed friends and allies were rendered unsympathetic by their anger. Rousseau held the book utterly detestable, and was aroused to write his Savoyard Vicar's profession of faith in defence of religion and morality.

De l'esprit was reprinted twenty times before the end of the year, mainly by foreign pirates. It was translated into English and German. Despite his fears, Helvétius was not physically molested, and was able to live out his days in Paris and at Voré until his death in 1771. He spent a lot of time in composing *De l'homme*, which was published after his death, a work which defended and developed the tenets of *De l'esprit*, and which was treated roughly by Diderot in his *Réfutation*, although he continued to hold *De l'esprit* one of the great books of the century, along with Montesquieu's *De l'esprit des lois* and Buffon's *Histoire naturelle*. Compared with those works, however, this tome of more than 600 pages lacks both the serenity and the sparkle which are essential to a book's survival. Instead it possesses a unique combination of loquacity and levity. Helvétius was a pupil of Fontenelle, and his book was evidently intended to continue the Fontenelle tradition. It succeeds only in proving the master's inimitability. Panting for literary fame, the author achieved only notoriety. He was in most respects his own worst enemy. Not only did he fail of the charm and freshness which still inform Fontenelle's *Entretiens* nearly three hundred years, but he egregiously overstated a rational half-truth. That self-preference generally governs human behaviour contains, as John Morley put it, a germ of wholesome doctrine, something that it is both foolish and impossible to attempt to disprove. To labour the point for hundreds of pages, even with the garnish of salacious anecdote and epigram, is to ensure oblivion.

Helvétius begins by reducing all men's intellectual faculties to a mechanical association of sense-impressions, the extreme form of the 'sensationalist' doctrine handled discreetly by Locke and Condillac. From this is deduced the total *tabula rasa* theory of mind. All the differences between men are then shown to be the product of their environment, the principal factors in this environment being legislation and education. From this is deduced an amoral and anti-ascetic scheme of ethics and politics based entirely on self-preference. Where previous thinkers of this school had rested content with tentative and empirical theories, Helvétius propounded an ideology. The whole scheme was directed to a programme of government whose proper name is 'utilitarian *étatisme*'. The most shocking section of the book is the Second Discourse which elaborates the hedonist or utilitarian ethics, the self-preference principle which governs the motivation of the individual in society, so that private vices produce public benefits in a coarser version of Mandeville's *Fable*. In chapter five the hedonist ethics are crudely overstated, with ample illustration by libertinist anecdote. The most outrageous example is the completely logical and revolting proposal that the choicest sexual enjoyment should be attached to the most socially valuable lines of action, so that presumably the intensest sexual satisfaction is to be the reward of the intensest public service. The fact that Helvétius himself was a well-known connoisseur of sexual pleasure should not affect the reader's approval, or otherwise, of this position, but it inevitably does, and no doubt it did at the time. Had he possessed even a *soupçon* of the austerity of a Bentham or a James Mill many of his teachings would probably have been less repellent.

The social utility of private vices easily conduces to a ready-made cynicism. Chapters seventeen and twenty-three of the Second Discourse, stating the single purpose of the laws and public policy to be the greatest happiness of the greatest number, and the ready equation of happiness with sensual satisfaction, provide us with the mainspring of Helvétius's theory of politics. The legislator's function is to compel men, by playing upon their sentiment of self-love, to be just to one another and to behave in socially useful ways. Helvétius entirely ignores the problem of self-love in the legislator himself, something which Bentham was to be greatly concerned with, and which ultimately led him to a belief in democratic government as the essential safeguard. In chapter twenty-four Helvétius gives a lurid picture of man's moral, and especially his religious, history. He evidently finds this necessary if he is to preclude religion as an effective basis for morality. Bentham, too, was intent on basing morality on personal interest, but before doing so he undertook a preliminary examination of possible alternatives, while refraining from turning religious history into the exhibition of a chamber of horrors. At least, we may concede, Helvétius was trying to base law and government upon observed, if distorted, facts. When he proceeds in his Third Discourse to assign all the intellectual differences between men to diversity of circumstances and specially of education, so that genius itself is made entirely dependent upon the individual's circumstances, in which education plays the dominant role, he reaches his most extreme and unconvincing position. To affirm that the man of genius is simply the product of fortunate circumstances; indeed, to avow that genius, so far from being a gift of nature, is a common quality, and that the only uncommon thing is the circumstantial situation favourable to its development: this was the perfect example of his fantastic overstatement of wholesome doctrine. He concludes with the assertion that the quality of everyone's intelligence is utterly dependent upon the government under which people live, and the times they live in, and most of all the education they receive.

Helvétius had, by the extreme behaviourist doctrine which he reached from the epistemological ideas of Locke as they had been acclimatised on French soil by such thinkers as Condillac, revealed to the *Philosophes* the revolutionary character of their cause. Bringing the philosophy of Locke and Condillac into the field of politics led to a full-dress attempt to think out and promote a totally utilitarian theory of government, equipped with the force and impetus required for social and political reconstruction. This no doubt is why John Morley thought that *De l'esprit*, despite its shallowness in many respects, contained the one principle which might have saved France from revolution. Certainly its widespread acceptance in England at the hands of the utilitarian radicals (along with the Wesleyan revival, no doubt) enabled England to make the transition from the *ancien régime* without upheaval. As it was, Helvétius's over-clever exaggeration of sound doctrine set both radicals and conservatives in France by the ears. Most of all its tone and tenor aroused opposition among people who should have been his allies, notably Diderot and the Encyclopedists. The sinister nature of his faith in an instructed minority who should bring the new dispensation, with their superstitious maxim 'education can do everything', drove them to denounce him as an advocate of enlightened despotism, or, as the twentieth century might prefer to say, of 'social engineering'. He was indeed the prophet of a peculiarly ruthless short-cut to salvation, the advocate of an *élite* of educated leaders who should dragoon the rest of mankind into the path of progress, the only begetter of the tyrannous minority of the modern state, either of the left or the right. Such by a fatal irony was the false and final flowering of the *Philosophe*.

And in case it should be imagined that Helvétius was the prophet of the Terror or a premature and private version of Robespierre, it should be added that he was personally a kind man who treated his seigniorial dependants generously and carried out his no doubt painful duties as a *fermier général* with mercy and consideration. Despite his fondness for sexual adventure he was a good husband and father. His wife, Anne-Catherine de Ligneville d'Autricourt, was a very beautiful woman and a Countess of the Holy Roman Empire. The little Élisabeth who danced with old Fontenelle was a pretty poppet. Claude-Adrien himself had none of the familial coldness which so often afflicts the do-gooder in personal relationships, though it is true that his friends stood aside somewhat ominously when his troubles broke upon him. Perhaps they found his panicky behaviour hard to bear in a *Philosophe*, generally speaking a tough and resilient race. Helvétius was physically round and robust, with melting eyes and lips that seemed to tremble upon the verge of tears. In fact he rather resembled the beaver in *The Hunting of the Snark*.

'No one man, perhaps, has done so much towards perfecting the theory of education as Mons. Helvétius', wrote James Mill who was, after Jeremy Bentham, the leading British utilitarian. He went on to ask why was Helvétius's works not more admired in his own country? Strangely, he ventured the explanation that 'it was too solid for the frivolous taste of the gay circles of Paris, assemblies of pampered *noblesse* who wished for nothing but amusement'. As for his reputation in Great Britain, it was said that his work was 'peculiarly dangerous to religion'. In fact, Mill declares, he never attacks religion, only priestcraft. As for his supposedly flippant style, 'there is nothing epigrammatic and sparkling in the expression'. He appeals only to the judgement and never attempts to delude through fancy. 'Nothing like a little judicious levity,' as Michael Finsbury said . . . But it was entirely lost on James Mill, who would not have cared for *The Wrong Box*. Of course, Mill may have been reading a rather dull English translation.

Chapter Eighteen

LE MAÎTRE D'HÔTEL DE LA PHILOSOPHIE

They are raining bombs on the house of the Lord . . . I go in fear and trembling lest one of these terrible bombers gets into difficulties.

DIDEROT to D'HOLBACH

THE German baron who lived in the Rue Royale⁄Saint⁄Roche spoke French like a Frenchman and had a Frenchman's taste for good food and wine. Every Sunday, and on most Thursdays, he entertained a large gathering of intellectuals from two to seven o'clock, and in fine summer weather he arranged philosophic picnics up the Seine or out at Grandval where he had an estate. Although he was an aggressive atheist he liked to take the company to the Embassy Chapel to hear their friend 'Sir Shandy Sterne' preach. Even David Hume would sometimes attend on these occasions, perhaps because he had seen John Wilkes there, and where Wilkes went David Hume could go.[1] Hume seems sometimes to have misinterpreted such things. 'Atheists?' he had exclaimed when he first sat down at the Baron's dinner⁄table. 'I don't believe there are any. I haven't met one . . .' Whereupon the Baron told him he had been somewhat unlucky, for out of the eighteen guests round the table fifteen were atheists and the other three hadn't quite made up their minds.

Paul Thiry, Baron d'Holbach was the son of an episcopal tax⁄farmer of the principality of Speyer who had migrated to Paris. The family prospered exceedingly in France, and soon they were not only naturalised Frenchmen but had adopted the 'de', at least with an apostrophe before the 'H'. Paul Thiry had been born at Edesheim and had gone to the University of Leyden where there were many Englishmen. After the

---

1 'I never see Mr Wilkes here but at Chapel, where he is a most regular and devout and edifying and pious Attendant. I take him to be entirely regenerate.' David Hume, writing home on 26 May 1764.

English fashion they had formed a 'Club', and when Paul moved to France it was transferred to Paris. The 'Synagogue d'Holbach', as it was known, was the natural resort of Englishmen visiting the capital. Hume, Wilkes, Sterne, Garrick, Dr Priestley, Lord Shelburne, Horace Walpole, all attended at one time or another. It was part of the intellectual exchange between the two countries which was such a prominent feature in the intellectual and social life of Europe in the eighteenth century. The Baron could well afford to entertain. He had £5,000 a year, which was a great deal of money in those days, and he employed it nobly to patronise the sciences. His library, his collection of drawings, his natural history cabinet, all were celebrated along with his dinner-parties. He was a genuine scholar, being a member of the princely Academies of Mann-heim, Petersburg and Berlin. His speciality was mineralogy. He was a first-class geologist and had written some 400 articles (mainly consisting of definitions) for the Encyclopedia. He wrote on metallurgical ques-tions, and the Baron's work on the extractive industries of France rivalled that of his friend Diderot on the handicrafts and manufactures. He also wrote on natural history and chemistry, besides composing some important articles on political questions like REPRÉSENTANTS.[1] He had a passion for anonymity. In publishing the names of contributors in the second volume, the editors of the Encyclopedia avowed their respect for this distinguished person's wish to remain anonymous, 'this philosopher-citizen who cultivates science with disinterestedness, without ambition, and in silence, and who, satisfied with the pleasure of being useful, does not even aspire to the legitimate glory of appearing so'. That the Baron should have wished to conceal the authorship of his atheistical books is understandable, but there was little likelihood of anyone scenting un-orthodox views in his writings on zinc or copper. His translation of German and Swedish scientific works into French – incidentally reveal-ing the secrets of the Saxon glassmakers to France – did much for French industry in his time.

The Synagogue d'Holbach, or the Café de l'Europe as it was often called, under the guidance and patronage of the '*Maître d'Hôtel de la Philosophie*', fulfilled a real need in the last years before the outbreak of the Revolution. Briefly, the salons of the famous lady-hostesses were no longer adequate to the changing age. Charming and chatty and unspecialised, they were neither masculine nor serious enough for the

---

[1] See *Revue d'histoire littéraire de la France*, 1951, pp. 330–2, for Professor Dieckmann's discoveries in the Fonds Vandeul bearing on d'Holbach's responsibility for various unsigned articles.

intellectual élite that planned to change the world, men who were not content to gossip about it. Nor was intellectual badinage so popular as it had been once. The eighteenth century, and especially France, was turning serious, not to say solemn, and the Baron was a German, after all. 'The dull Baron d'Holbach's' Horace Walpole called the Synagogue, or 'a pigeon-house' of authors, savants and philosophers. Horace was now sixty-five and growing deaf. He couldn't bear it. He longed for the good old days of Madame du Deffand.[1] When Marmontel, on the other hand, came to write his memoirs he welcomed the fact that the Baron's parties were more virile, the rendezvous of people who would have been too venturesome and even risky for the great ladies' tables. At d'Holbach's 'we were no longer tied to a woman's apron-strings'. Suard, writing about 1820, stresses the importance of the rare alliance of opulence and philo-sophy in Parisian society in general, and at the house of the Baron in particular. He regards this as the indispensable condition which alone enabled the Age of Reason to bring forth the Revolution, though he deplores the latter as a revolution in which 'truth inflamed the passions without enlightening the mind'. D'Holbach's synagogue was a 'general institute' at a time when there were only 'particular academies'. It pro-vided a clearing-house for specialists in an atmosphere of generality. Members of various academies mingled there. The Baron was a kind of Seneca. He read books that men like Diderot needed to use, telling them what they contained and saving them the labour of reading them.

The later salons, more especially those of d'Holbach and Helvétius, had a distinctly middle-class inclination towards all things English. More formal and even pedantic than their predecessors, they were certainly more political in tone. Most striking of all in these respects was the *Entre-sol* which had its headquarters above Madame de Pompadour's apartment in Versailles itself. There Madame, herself often present at the discussions, housed François Quesnay, the economist, and there assembled the Physiocrats. As Marmontel says, they thought and talked nothing from morn to night but politics and political economy. There one might meet Helvétius, Diderot, d'Alembert, Duclos, Buffon and Turgot, all men concerned with changing the world and not merely 'explaining it' as Marx was to distinguish them when he spoke of the historical function of the *Philosophes*.

The French theatre, too, was undergoing a change at this time with the invasion of the stage by bourgeois and even peasant drama, especially

[1] He did not cross the Channel again after her death in 1780.

at the hands of Beaumarchais with *Le Barbier de Séville* and *Le Mariage de Figaro. Opéra comique* parodied the opera proper with its courtly, aristocratic, artificial style. Now as the 'Apostles of Equality' began to make the theatre the organ of social criticism once more – in the old tradition of Molière – the Count and his servant were set face to face, and Figaro came off as the better man. With the introduction of the bourgeois and the peasant figures the whole social system had won right of entry on to the comic stage.

When the Baron began to turn out books, which he commenced to do in earnest in 1765, he published thirty in ten years, many of them under the names of the illustrious dead, such as Nicolas Fréret and J. D. Mirabaud, both of whom had departed this life before the Baron came to Paris. The reason for this great rush into print was his conversion to atheism by Diderot in 1763 and his need to convert everyone else, or at least to take his revenge upon the religion which had deluded him for so long. He had all the fanaticism of the convert. Nearing forty, he had seen the light rather as St Paul's eyes were opened on the road to Damascus, and as St Paul fell down a persecutor and rose up an apostle, so Paul Thiry fell down a deist and rose up an atheist. He transferred his proselytism to the new cause for the remainder of his life, and *Le Système de la nature*, which he published under the name of Mirabaud in 1770, made sufficient noise in the world to puzzle the young Goethe how a book 'so dark, so Cimmerian, so death‑like' could possibly be danger‑ ous. It also had the honour of being attacked by the two most distin‑ guished atheists in Europe.[1] Voltaire attacked it for both its style and its content. It belonged, he said, to 'the boring genre', and it is true that the Baron's prose was extremely stodgy. And how absurd, Voltaire exclaimed, to write a fanatical book against fanaticism. How inconsistent to combine a belief in necessity and an attack on priests and kings for being what necessity had made them, said Frederick. 'What foolishness and what nonsense . . . One might as well preach to an oak and try to persuade it to turn into an orange‑tree.' Nevertheless, *Le Système* had an immense popularity *de choc*. It did especially well when it came out in abbreviated form under the title *Le Bon‑sens (ou idées naturelles opposées aux idées surnaturelles)*, in 1772.

Before he produced *Le Système*, the Baron had served as literary executor to Nicolas Boulanger (1722–59), a civil engineer who had played an important part in the planning and construction of the great

---

[1] 'Thus God had the two least superstitions men in Europe on his side,' said Voltaire, 'which must have pleased him very much.'

highways which were built in France in the first part of the eighteenth
century and which Arthur Young was to praise so highly in his celebrated
Travels in the years 1787-9, even while he was amazed that they were so
little frequented. Boulanger, at his premature death, was engaged on a
work on Oriental despotism. D'Holbach brought this out in 1761 with
a prefatory letter to Helvétius deploring the way he had injured the
Encyclopedists by shocking mankind with philosophical paradoxes and
generalisations before they had been accustomed to the facts of history.
Boulanger's fragment on Oriental despotism, it is explained, was intended
to introduce a work on man's history in society from the earliest times
comparable to Voltaire's Essai sur les mœurs. A second work by Nicolas
Boulanger, L'Antiquité dévoilée par ses usages, was kept back until 1765,
and in the meantime d'Holbach fathered on him his own 'Christianisme
dévoilé', another fanatical exposure, much inferior to the deceased
author's own work. Perhaps d'Holbach thought the name of the author
of the fragment on Oriental despotism would serve better to pass off his
anti-Christian propaganda. The interesting thing about Boulanger's
work is its debt to his experience as a civil engineer which had revealed
to him 'the archives of the earth', very much as the making of railway-
cuttings in the nineteenth century was to serve the science of geology
with the unearthing of fossils. At any rate, the earth's archives set
Boulanger thinking on a great thesis: that man's early history in religion
and mythology was to be explained in terms of fear – the experience and
apprehension of the great calamities of nature, more especially the
Flood. Boulanger contributed an article on DÉLUGE to the Encyclopedia,
and this proved the germ of the more ambitious L'Antiquité dévoilée par
ses usages on which he was engaged at the time of his death in 1759, and
which d'Holbach published as his literary executor in 1765. Horace
Walpole was fond of poking fun at him for it, talking of 'a new system
of antediluvian deluges' which was 'invented to prove the eternity
of matter'. The Baron, he said, was persuaded that Pall Mall is paved
with lava or deluge-stones. Perhaps he had something to do with the
nickname for the Baron's household at this time: 'La Grande Boulan-
gerie'.

   Baron d'Holbach's offensive for the destruction of Christianity, 'the
sacred poison', or religion in general, really opened with his publication
of Boulanger's L'Antiquité dévoilée, and it occupied him for the next
ten years, the decade in which he brought out some thirty books devoted
to the cause, nearly all of them under other people's names, and every
one of them dull. The content of his atheism, best represented in Le

Système de la nature, could have been set down on a single sheet of note⁄
paper. Its heads are as follows:

Things are what they seem.
The senses, and nothing else, are to be relied on.
There is a single objective reality, of which all our knowledge is gained
by our senses.
This reality is matter imbued with motion, and there is nothing else.
Matter is not 'caused'. It exists from eternity to eternity, causeless
and necessary.
Man is a function of matter: a part of the universal and objective
substance, completely necessitated.
Like everything else, he has neither free⁄will nor 'soul'.
His notions of freedom and spirituality are illusions.
He is like a walking plant or a tree.
Religion is a trick men play on one another, for the profit of the
cunning. It is a 'sacred poison', injurious to mind and body, socially
disastrous, but useful to those who govern. It might be called (though
the Baron does not use the phrase) 'the opium of the people'.
The task of philosophy is to unmask the poisoners, to get the poison
out of the social system.
Atheism is not an 'alternative' nor a 'criticism', it is a duty of social
hygiene.

'We laughed him out,' says Goethe after renouncing this death⁄like
book, for the author had said that he was an old man, just sinking into
the grave, and 'we had observed that by old people nothing in the world
that is lovable and good is in fact appreciated'. He said that all was
to be of necessity, and therefore there was no God. 'But could there
not be a God by necessity too?' asked we. After admitting the neces⁄
sities of day and night, the seasons, the climate, physical and animal
conditions,

nevertheless we felt within us something that appeared like perfect
freedom of will . . . The hope of becoming more and more rational,
of making ourselves more and more independent of external things,
nay, of ourselves, we could not give up. The word freedom sounds so
beautiful, that we cannot do without it, even though it designates an
error.

Thus young Goethe, thus all young creatures, all creatures in whom the
spirit of life and love and joy is moving. The Baron had to be left to his

senility, hugging his *système*. If, after all, the book 'did us any mischief', Goethe reflected when he looked back,

> it was this – that we took a hearty dislike to all philosophy, and especially metaphysics, and remained in that dislike; while on the other hand we threw ourselves into living knowledge, experience, action, and poetising, with all the more liveliness and passion.

So did the Baron himself, if we omit the poetising. The household out at Grandval, where Diderot passed so many happy days away from the toil of the Encyclopedia, was one of the liveliest in France in those last days of the dying régime. It was made the more lively by the Baron's remarkable old mother-in-law, Madame d'Aine. When her first daughter died, the Baron got a dispensation to enable him to marry the second, so well did he love the brood. When this pioneer of the deceased-wife's-sister bill departed this life in the year of the French Revolution, he was buried in the parish church of Saint-Roche in Paris, despite all his dreadful works. There, in the Chapel of the Virgin, behind the high altar, he lies side by side with his old friend Diderot. The naturalistic materialist and the dogmatic atheist lie there with their toes pointing up to heaven, though without a memorial tablet between them, St Denis and St Paul. Thus, somehow, the ancient Church gathers in her glorious dead. After all, the Baron's books never mattered very much, but the Synagogue was one of the most important seed-beds of the coming Revolution.

Chapter Nineteen

ROUSSEAU

You are too rich.

ROUSSEAU to D'HOLBACH

JEAN-JACQUES ROUSSEAU belongs to a work on the *Philosophes* only by way of contrast. To study this *promeneur solitaire* is to discover all the things the *Philosophes* were not. From such a study he emerges the more individualistic, even idiosyncratic, while they appear in the common character which unites *hommes engagés* in all ages. Just for a little while, in the days of his youth, Rousseau appears to have been, if not a member of the sect at any rate a friend of some of its members. A passage in the Seventh Book of his *Confessions* describes his early intimacy with Condillac, Diderot and d'Alembert at the time when the Encyclopedia was beginning. He tells us how he was invited to write the articles on music, how he accepted, how he laid out time and money on the task, and how he met with no financial recompense. 'Diderot had promised me on behalf of the booksellers a fee, which he has never mentioned to me again; nor have I mentioned it to him.'

There follows Rousseau's famous account of how he went to visit Diderot at Vincennes. He professes to have been deeply distressed on account of 'poor Diderot's' hardships, even to have asked to be imprisoned with him. No notice was taken of this request. Instead, Rousseau went on foot to the fortress on a very hot summer's day, being too poor to afford a cab. It was on the way thither that he read in *Le Mercure de France* of the prize offered by the University of Dijon for an essay on the question whether the progress of the arts and sciences had done more to corrupt morals or to improve them. When he got to Vincennes he was so moved by inspiration for the essay that he was, he says, 'in a state of agitation bordering on delirium'. Of course, Diderot wanted to know what was the matter, and from the moment when Rousseau told him their friendship was threatened with shipwreck. What precisely were the rights and wrongs of the matter it is impossible to make out. As we saw earlier[1] Diderot was to record himself as having persuaded Rousseau to write against the beneficial effects of the progress of the arts and sciences. To take the *per contra* view would enable him to be really original and eloquent. Anyway, as he was to say many years later, 'Rousseau *had* to disagree with everyone else.' But Rousseau got it firmly and for ever into his head that he came to his decision himself and owed little or nothing of the essay to Diderot, and moreover that Diderot was always determined to take the credit to himself, more especially when – after having for‹ gotten all about his essay – Rousseau heard, in 1750, that he had won the prize. In the *Confessions* he says that from the moment Diderot gave him his advice, and he put in for the competition, 'I was lost. All the rest of my life and of my misfortunes followed inevitably as a result of that moment's madness.'

What precisely does he mean – if anything, apart from a typical piece of Rousseauite drama? Can he have intended us to believe that all his life's suffering followed upon his having chosen the wrong side on that hot summer's afternoon in 1749? 'All my little passions', he says, recount‹ ing how he wrote the essay, 'were stifled by an enthusiasm for truth, liberty and virtue', which was to work in his heart for more than four or five years 'as intensely perhaps as it has ever worked in the heart of any man on earth'. It must surely be apparent to us, as it certainly was to himself, that he had chosen the right side – the side of 'truth, liberty, and virtue' – in choosing to condemn the influence of the arts and sciences. For he had engaged in a wholesale condemnation of advancing civilisa‹ tion. When he produced his second essay five years later, on the Origins of Inequality, Voltaire was right to call it Rousseau's 'second book against the human race'. He had taken his side before he was forty, and it was not the side of the *Philosophes*. The only thing he could say to the *Maître d'Hôtel de la Philosophie*, when d'Holbach offered to help him, was – by his own confession – 'You are too rich.' He was to write on a great number of things in the next thirty years, botany, political economy, the theatre, political institutions, but he was really writing always about one thing: the corruption of man, whether at the hands of material progress, the deplorable institutions of the *ancien régime*, or the modern 'great state' which, with its representative institutions and its sovereignty of the majority, denied liberty and democracy as completely as any despotic prince. Were there a people of gods, he said in *Du contrat social*, its government would be democratic, but such a government is not for men. Did he want better bread than can be made from wheat, as

1 See above, p. 63.

Thomas De Quincey once said of Coleridge? That is what religious
revolutionaries are prone to want, and Rousseau was both religious and
revolutionary. It was to the extent that his inspiration was religious that
he was revolutionary in a way that the *Philosophes* were not, and that his
impact upon European history was that of a religious thinker. What the
Reformation had been to the Renaissance, Rousseau was to the *Philosophes*.

Their divergence was at root religious. To him it seemed that they
grossly overestimated the power of reason and knowledge in human
nature. Like Burke, whom he resembled in many ways unacknowledged
in his century, and largely unsuspected since, he knew that 'man is by
his constitution a religious animal'. To the *Philosophes* political problems,
indeed all problems, were best solved by treating religion as negligible.
Theirs was an age when religion was suffering from the dead weight of
institutionalism, and that hardening of the arteries which accompanies
the freezing of the spirit by the letter. It was an age which, while it did
not say 'God is dead', greatly hoped and believed that He was rapidly
dying. Any man who greatly cared for the things of the spirit was driven
to look elsewhere than to churches for hope. Rousseau, shuddering in
the cold blasts of the Age of Reason, was driven to a divinised Nature.
Before his remains were removed to the Panthéon in 1794, they rested in
the Temple of the Philosophers at Ermenonville, memorialised by a
column inscribed *Naturam*. Everything that Goethe said of d'Holbach's
grey and spectral book, *Le Système de la nature*, might have been said by
Jean-Jacques Rousseau half a century and more earlier. He, not Goethe,
was the true father of Romanticism.

When Burke called Rousseau 'a hollow logician' he was saying the
reverse of the truth. It is true there were certain vestigial remains of the
Philosophe spirit about his more didactic writings, for he was impelled to
try and prove his fundamental tenets true, and to lay out his arguments
in a rigidly logical way. But for the logical exigencies of the French
language he might as well have rested content with Pascal's aphorism:
'The heart has its reasons which reason cannot know.' His hankering
after logical exposition was at least in part his instinctive response to the
nature of his age and the society to which he addressed himself. It was
also a consequence of his never having part or parcel in politics or
government. Like most excluded prophets he was always tempted to
have recourse to logic instead of experience. But the impact of his
teachings was rarely restricted to the type of impact which comes from
logical persuasion. Infinitely more important than any pattern of rational
discourse are the moral force of his vision and the unapprehended power

of the language in which he clothed it. *Du contrat social* with its curiously theorometric attempt to answer the question: what can make the chains of law legitimate, so that man can live in the chains of civil society, and yet 'remain as free as before'? – this highly ingenious, not to say didactic thesis, provides modern man with the moral apology for democracy and the source of the theory of the modern state. It is something which the *Philosophes*, with all their clarity and wit, never approached, indeed seem never to have dreamt of. The opening words of the book, 'Man is born free, and yet is everywhere in chains', strike a perfectly new and different note. They are the first words of eighteenth,century France to bear the stamp of immortality, even though the future was to mistake their import because, like so many of man's favourite quotations, they were generally taken out of context. Have any of the many thousands of words of the self,accredited *Philosophes* a tittle of their memorability in the mind of Western man? They have some of the mysterious force of the words which the world has possessed for twenty centuries from the acts of the Christian apostles. They resound like a deed, a blow struck upon men's hearts.

Chapter Twenty

THE MARQUIS'S OMELETTE

IN England a marquis comes somewhere between a duke and an earl. In old France he was a count. Voltaire once said that in France anyone who wanted to could become a marquis, by which he meant that, like many other titles, it went with some office or other, and since a great many offices could be bought there was no guarantee that a marquis was either of ancient family or of great estates. Condorcet was of ancient family, but his father, captain of a regiment of the Barbançon cavalry, lived in a dull little house in the dull little town of Ribemont in Picardy. It was a place where 'people didn't know how to read or write', where the people offered up masses when the cattle died of disease and refused to import butcher's meat in case they should catch it. The young Condorcet went round from stable to stable trying to do something about it with a veterinary student. The future disciple of the Encyclopedists believed in action, for it was characteristic of *le bon* Condorcet to live close to the people and concern himself with their problems.

He went to the Jesuit College of Navarre in Paris, and he soon showed a decided preference for science, although like the sons of the Caritat family he took it for granted that he was to serve the army or the church. 'The only one up to now who could forgive me for not being a priest or a cavalry officer,' he once said in commending one of his relations. Marie-Jean-Antoine-Nicolas Caritat published a little book on the integral calculus instead. It greatly pleased Jean le Rond d'Alembert. Mathematicians spoke of him in the same breath with Descartes, Pascal, Leibniz and Newton, and in 1769, when he was twenty-six, he was elected to the Académie des Sciences. A few years later he became its perpetual secretary, with the duty of composing its *éloges* in the tradition of Fontenelle, which he performed with a fine tact and discretion. According to Diderot, 'He brought their good points into full daylight and painted their defects in half-tones.' His generosity was matched only by his frankness and promptitude in avowing his own defects. When relations with Diderot had become strained, he was heard to say that

Diderot was the best of men and that one was always in the wrong in quarrelling with him.

'And what about you?' someone asked.

'I was wrong,' Condorcet replied simply.

Julie de Lespinasse, who made him her close friend and did much to bring him out when he went to live in Paris, said that 'goodness' was his chief characteristic. 'This calm and moderate soul only became fierce and full of fire when defending the oppressed or the unfortunate; then his zest amounted to passion; he was hot and tormented.' Julie seems to have thought of him as one of the rather nicer saints. Of all the *Philosophes* he is the only one of whom can be employed the word 'noble', without a suspicion of sententiousness. He was an aristocrat in the Greek sense of *aristos*, or 'the best'. It did much to destroy him at a time when the word had acquired a pejorative sense. Even in his life it appears to have led some people to call him a courtier, mainly because they misheard the name Condorcet for 'Comte d'Orsay'.

His career was not, as has sometimes been imagined, that of a mathematician who turned to political and social problems. Rather it was his lifelong endeavour to bring science, indeed mathematics itself, to the solution of the problems of his time. He conceived it possible for the men of the eighteenth century to tackle their problems with the tools put at their disposal by the great scientific advances of the seventeenth. That is the inspiration of his famous *Esquisse*, written in the shadow of the guillotine and published after his death. A specialised preamble of this work, written for his fellow-academicians, was published ten years earlier under the title of *Essai sur l'application de l'analyse*. Its purpose was to persuade them that the moral and political sciences can best be treated mathematically. After 1793, when the Revolution was in full spate, he published a statement of precisely the same contention in a more popular form entitled: 'A general view of the science which comprises the mathematical treatment of the moral and political sciences.' The link between the higher mathematics and the treatment of social problems was 'the calculus of probabilities'. All statements of experience were to be expressed and adjudged in terms of the theory of probability. In this Condorcet was mathematically a Cartesian and sociologically very close to Giambattista Vico with his attempt to establish the validity of social science. In the *Essai sur l'application de l'analyse* he attempted to show how the calculus of probabilities could enable us to discover whether the majority decisions of an assembly (*les décisions rendues à la pluralité des voix*, as the longer title puts it) are true. It would enable us to reconcile the claims of an élite to be responsible for decision-making with the general principle of universal, or majority, consent.

Despite its somewhat clumsy, complicated, even obscure mathe-matical apparatus, this remarkable work has afforded later scholars an interesting model of collective decision for the study of the relationships between individual and collective choice. The pioneer work of Con-dorcet in a field which has only become important to sociological enquiry with the growth of populous 'democracies' and their problems of de-cision-making, has been recognised somewhat late in the twentieth century. In his own day it had something to do with the failure of acceptance of the Girondin constitution of 1793. For him to have canvassed such com-plicated and scientific proposals at the moment when France was in moral danger and submitting herself to the command of the Committee of Public Safety suggests in Condorcet a singular, if momentary, lack of political sense or realism. It was the dream of a *Philosophe*. He did not, however, regard his *mathématique sociale* as an academic exercise but as a 'common and ordinary science', the future foundation of democratic and national politics, a politics liberated from the blind instincts of the gambler, conducted in the light of reason and precise calculation. Social mathematics, coupled with an exact language, would provide us with the link between scientific advance and social progress. Most evils, he held, are more the result of a failure correctly to calculate the consequences of our actions than of our insubordinate passions. In 1793, however, the insubordinate passions seemed to be having things all their own way. The *Philosophe* and his constitution were shoved aside by the avalanche of history.

Condorcet, however, was an active participant in public affairs not only during the Revolution but during the twenty years leading up to it. When Turgot was Controller-General, in 1774-6, Condorcet – along with other friends and fellow-reformers – was taken into the public service. The office of the Marquis de Condorcet was that of *Inspecteur des Monnaies*, or overseer of the mint. He was not a rich man, and Turgot might see to it – as Julie de Lespinasse said – that 'the good Condorcet should have soup and chops every day at home'. He wrote a number of brochures at this time dealing mainly with the problem of peasant poverty and the beneficial effects of Turgot's reformist policy of freer trade in grain and the reduction of impositions like the forced labour which crippled the peasant. His knowledge of, and sympathy with, the people of his own countryside may be discovered in his *Lettre du laboureur de Picardie* addressed to Necker and begging to know, in a

spirit of raillery, whether there can be anything either wrong or danger‹
ous in the people knowing the truth about speculators and the trade in
grain? Do you believe, sir, that it would be dangerous to allow the
people to emerge from their ignorance, or that man becomes bad when
he becomes enlightened?

With the fall of Turgot we find him bidding him farewell thus:'Fare‹
well my dear and illustrious master, we have had a beautiful dream, but
it was too brief. I shall go and devote myself to geometry and philosophy
where one may be appreciated for giving of one's time for the good of
society.' He continued to write on public questions, however, especially
as he watched with enthusiasm the revolt of the American Colonies
against the King of England, and the establishment of their republican
constitution. His *Lettres d'un gentilhomme à MM. du Tiers État* reveals
in every line how this man, 'born into the nobility and brought up by
the Encyclopedia', was devoted to the cause of the people. As for the
King of England, robbed of his subjects by revolt, Condorcet, like many
Frenchmen, rehearsed his sentiments of later years towards the monarchy
of his own country. He was prepared to admit that 'his person is sacred',
but only because he was 'the repository of all the citizens' power to
ensure that the laws were carried out'. He was, as he proved by his
refusal to vote for the death‹sentence of Louis XVI, ideally republican
while he remained 'in practice a monarchist'.

He married Sophie Marie‹Louise de Grouchy, daughter of the Mar‹
quis de Grouchy who brought him the Château de Villette. There and at
Paris the marquis and his lady presided over one of the most lively salons
of the *ancien régime*. When the Revolution broke out, Condorcet was a
member of the Municipal Council of Paris, and in 1791 he was a leading
member of the Legislative Assembly. Here he was to play the preponder‹
ating role in its Comité d'Instruction Publique, for whose deliberations
he framed five *mémoires* which set out a complete system. The primary
principle is contained in the statement: 'Public instruction is a duty
which society owed to the citizen.' Secondly, such education was to be
free, and to be imparted to both boys and girls 'in mixed schools'.
There was to be complete liberty of conscience, and no 'official doctrine'.
The grades of schools envisaged are, at the base of the system the
primaire, then the *primaire supérieur*, and lastly what today is called the
post‹scolaire, including evening classes and adult education. The breadth
and imagination which were shown in the third *mémoire* dealing with the
post‹scolaire education is remarkable for the time, but not surprising in
a disciple of the Encyclopedists whose great work had always been

concerned with 'adult education'. Condorcet's comprehensive scheme is really the basic model of public instruction in the Third Republic. Unfortunately it was not implemented in his own time, for on the day when he presented it to the Legislative Assembly, the proceedings were disrupted by the arrival of Louis XVI's proposal for declaration of war on Austria (20 April 1792) which opened the long course of the Revolutionary Wars.

With the War and the Terror, Condorcet's party, the Girondins were fated to give way to the Jacobins. The Girondin Constitution was rejected by the Convention, one of its most objectionable features being – according to the radicals on the 'Mountain' – 'the frightfully slow and complicated' system of election. Certainly the mechanism was complicated; for alongside the representative organs of government, Condorcet had given 'an important place to direct rule, that is to say to the intervention of the citizens gathered together in primary assemblies.' These last could approve, or otherwise, the constitution, demand its revision, exercise a right of censure over legislation, even dissolve the legislative body in accordance with a referendum. All these complicated provisions were part and parcel of his endeavour to bring 'social mathematics' to bear, in accordance with his *Essai sur l'application de l'analyse*. This was the inspiration of the complicated machinery of the Girondin constitution. Its failure doomed the party. The Jacobins were now in the ascendant. Condorcet was proscribed and went into hiding. His situation was the more perilous because Robespierre held him in both personal and ideological detestation. 'The Sea-green Incorruptible' had reason to believe that he had been given his nickname by Condorcet's appending of the word *'l'incorruptible'* to the signature 'Maximilien Robespierre' at the foot of a mock-letter in the *Chronique de Paris*. He had, too, an abiding hatred of the Encyclopedists whom he persisted in publicly describing as 'a sect', and most wicked of all the sect which had persecuted the god of Robespierre's idolatry, Jean-Jacques Rousseau. He regarded Condorcet as a man in whom to strike down the aristocrat, the savant, the atheist, the man who mocked at his gods in the name of an implacable rejection of all dogmatism and superstition, including that of the Supreme Being of whom Robespierre accounted himself the chief priest, not to mention the *État-Dieu*. Most telling of all in appealing to the vulgar mind against the old enemy was his status as the former Marquis Condorcet.

For eight months he lived in hiding in the house of the widow of the sculptor François Vernet in the Rue des Fossayeurs. There it was, in a first-floor room over the courtyard, that he was to spend the last days of his life (he was little more than fifty at his death) writing his *Esquisse d'un tableau historique des progrès de l'esprit humain*. For a number of years he had contemplated a comprehensive work on the history of science and its impact on society. Now time was short. He was a hunted man. He would write the sketch as an introduction to the larger work which was unlikely ever to be written. It might serve as only – or nothing less than – the testament of the *Philosophe*. Despite its notably personal character-istics, it does still serve as that. It is a monument to a mind and an age, the mind of mankind – and especially French mankind – in one of its great celebrations of rationality and optimism.

The aim of the work is stated at the beginning:

> to show by appeal to reason and fact that nature has set no term to the perfection of the human faculties; that the perfectibility of man is truly indefinite; and that the progress of his perfectibility, from now onwards independent of any power which might wish to halt it, has no other limit than the duration of the globe upon which nature has cast us.

This progress was necessarily very slow and not of equal speed in all places. For long periods, especially the Dark and the Middle Ages, it was a matter of creeping and crawling. The great age of progress, for Con-dorcet, is *now*. It has been accelerating since the time of the Renaissance, and especially since Bacon and Descartes and Newton, and the birth of modern science. How does he get over the difficulty of bringing light out of darkness, the difficulty which always confronts the thinker who accepts the apocalyptic view of history, the sudden dawn of light in a dark world? To ascribe the coming of the Renaissance to the westward disper-sion of culture by the Turkish invasions of Byzantium in the fifteenth century had been good enough for Voltaire, just as he had been prepared to accept Pascal's attribution of vital significance, for world history, to the length of Cleopatra's nose. To regard some single fact or event, however seemingly important, as having the force of a *deus ex machina*, was far too naïve for Condorcet. Instead, he finds the mainspring of progress in our errors and prejudices. As Marx was to make the oppres-sion of the workers essential to the development of class-consciousness and the emergence of revolution, so Condorcet argues that 'according to the general laws of the development of our faculties, certain prejudices have necessarily come into being at each stage of our progress . . .' These prejudices have lasted long beyond their due season 'because men retain the prejudices of their childhood, their country and their age, long after they have discovered all the truths necessary to destroy them'. Different prejudices afflict (and benefit) different countries in different ages. The prejudices of philosophers harm the progress of truth. The prejudices of certain powerful professions have arrested the progress of technology. Even the unenlightened poor play a part in the provision of these stimulating obstacles. But the most powerful and persistent obstacles are the castes of priests, secular and sacerdotal, whose interest it is to keep the mass of mankind in darkness and ignorance in order to retain their own sovereignty. Taking possession of education they make men content with their chains, and destroy their desire to break them. Their role, however, is only apparently unprogressive. It is needed in order to provoke the requisite activity in the energetic part of mankind which will overthrow them and bring the next stage of progress. We have now reached this stage. The present state of enlightenment assures us that *this* revolution will have a favourable result. To be sure of this, 'do we not need to study the history of the human spirit to discover what obstacles we still have to fear and what means are open to us of surmount‑ ing them?' That is what the *Esquisse* is intended to do.

Herein is to be found the principle of action which governs Condor‑ cet's portrait of the *progrès de l'esprit humain*. The actual stages through which this progress has gone are less important, or at any rate less original, for Voltaire, d'Alembert and Turgot had all schematised history in much the same pattern, arriving at the eighteenth century as at the dawn of enlightenment, the dayspring of a yet brighter hereafter. All had been concerned with history, very much as he was, as what Voltaire called the record of the crimes and follies of mankind, but only Condor‑ cet had discovered in such crimes and follies a vital term in the dialectic of progress, and thus could take a really philosophic view of the long story of man's misery. He finds nine of these stages, the ninth and latest being that from Descartes to the foundation of the French Republic. Ancient Greece gets a stage to itself (the fourth), but Rome gets only the accidental achievements of the Christian Empire of the Middle Ages. The Christian centuries are divided at the Crusades, when there began the revival of knowledge which was to culminate in the invention of printing. From that point knowledge was at length indestructible, and science, shaking off the yoke of authority, could progress to the ninth stage – in which men still live. The history of man through these stages is 'linked by an uninterrupted chain of facts and observations; so that at this point the picture of the march and progress of the human mind becomes truly historical'. This is the counterpart of Marx's transition from the ages of necessity to those of liberty – man's emergence into history proper.

When, after studying man's progress through the eight stages, and his arrival in the ninth, when 'the progress of the human mind becomes truly historical', then and only then 'philosophy has nothing more to guess, no more hypothetical surmises to make; it is enough to assemble and order the facts and to show the useful truths that can be derived from their connections and from their totality'. All that remains is to employ the past for the extrapolation of the future, to sketch the final picture: 'that of our hopes, and of the progress reserved for future generations, which the constancy of the laws of nature seems to assure them. This is the whole point of the *Esquisse*: the assurance that present error and prejudice are transitory, that truth alone will obtain a lasting victory'. What could have seemed more heart-warming to the hunted man, the former marquis, writing, writing, writing, in the shadow of the guillotine? For the greatest and most splendid-promising revolution in human history was eating its children, degenerating into a monster. It was this philosophic comfort that consoled the English poets Coleridge and Wordsworth, mainly at the hands of Condorcet's disciple, William Godwin, in the aftermath of the Terror. The final exordium, though it comes in the introduction to the work, must be cited:

> We shall demonstrate how nature has joined together indissolubly the progress of knowledge and that of liberty, virtue, and respect for the natural rights of man; and how these, the only real goods we possess, though so often separated that they have even been held to be incompatible, must on the contrary become inseparable from the moment when enlightenment has attained a certain level in a number of nations, and has penetrated throughout the whole mass of a great people whose language is universally known and whose commercial relations embrace the whole area of the globe. Once such a close accord had been established between all enlightened men, from then onwards all will be the friends of humanity, all will work together for its perfection and its happiness.

When he does come, quite literally, to the final paragraph of his sketch, Condorcet shows himself to be the true *Philosophe* of the Diderot tradition in his recourse to the secular tradition of immortality – the sole brand of immortality the *Philosophe* could hope for.

> How consoling for the philosopher who laments the errors, the crimes, the injustices which still pollute the earth and of which he is often the victim, is this view of the human race emancipated from its shackles, released from the empire of fate and from that of the enemies of its

F

progress, advancing with a firm and sure step along the path of truth, virtue and happiness! It is the contemplation of this prospect that rewards him for all his efforts to assist the progress of reason and the defence of liberty. He dares to regard these strivings as part of the eternal chain of human destiny; and in this persuasion he is filled with the true delight of virtue and the pleasure of having done some lasting good which fate can never destroy by a sinister stroke of revenge, by calling back the reign of slavery and prejudice. Such contemplation is for him an asylum, in which the memory of his persecutors cannot pursue him; there he lives in thought with man restored to his natural rights and dignity, forgets man tormented and corrupted by greed, fear or envy; there he lives with his peers in an Elysium created by reason and graced by the purest pleasures known to the love of mankind.

Few things in history are more moving than this hymn to the inevit‑ able perfectibility of man, sung by the Marquis de Condorcet before he left his lodging with Madame Vernet and wandered out into the French countryside to die. He had overheard the intentions of his pursuers as they visited the adjoining rooms, and he had received warnings from friends. He would not bring peril to those who had harboured him.

He was weary and famished when he came to the inn at Clamart‑le‑ Vignoble. There he is said to have ordered an omelette, though it is thought unlikely that he indulged in the fatal extravagance of ordering an omelette of twelve eggs which is sometimes said to have betrayed his aristocratic rank. As one biographer has said, with the unfortunate anxiety of the historian to spoil a good story: 'How should he have known how many eggs to break in order to make an omelette suited to his appetite?'[1] Suspicion is just as likely to have been aroused by his elegant manners and his long white hands, 'hands which had never worked much, in a word – the hands of an aristocrat'. Anyway, they carried him to Bourg‑la‑Rein (latterly renamed Bourg‑Égalité) in a wine‑dresser's cart. Before the friends of man, marching remorselessly towards their inevitable perfectibility, could send him to the guillotine, he was found by his jailer, dead in his cell. It seems likely that he had taken poison, and no one knows where his remains lie, for the cemetery at Bourg‑Égalité no longer exists, though there is still a Place Condorcet.

---

[1] As a Frenchman, a specialist in the mathematics of calculation, and like all Frenchmen a culinary expert, it seems likely that the Marquis *did* ask for '*Omelette à douze.*'

EPILOGUE

THE *Philosophes* were characteristic of the Enlightenment in somewhat the same way as the pig's pizzler that Arabella Donn threw at Jude Fawley was (as Hardy is careful to explain), 'the characteristic part of the barrow-pig'. They were similarly a symbol of vitality, and generally regarded as no less disgusting. Hardly was their day done, when '*Philosophe*' became a dirty word. 'What may you be?' a Dane asked Coleridge on the Yarmouth–Hamburg packet in 1798. 'A *Philosophe* perhaps?' 'I was at that time of my life,' says Coleridge, 'in which of all possible names and characters I had the greatest disgust to that of *un Philosophe*.' When the Dane began to rant like Tom Paine in *The Age of Reason*, Coleridge at once assumed a serious look, whereupon 'I sank a hundred fathoms in his good graces.' Another case is that of Thomas De Quincey's mother. Living in the neighbourhood of Manchester, she made the acquaintance of a certain Dr P, 'a literary man of elegant tastes and philosophic habits', who sought to interest her in his correspondents in France, Voltaire, Diderot, Maupertuis, Condorcet and d'Alembert, men 'who cultivated literature jointly with philosophy'. When Mrs De Quincey heard Dr P. extol these gentlemen she at once assumed that 'being a philosopher he must be an infidel'. Poor Dr P.'s reputation was quickly blasted. 'In spite of his Buffon, his Diderot, his d'Alembert . . . whose frothy letters he kept like amulets in his pocket-book, he ranked in general esteem as no better than one of the sons of the feeble.' All this was within less than half a century of Diderot's article in the Encyclo-pedia. The name of *Philosophe* has never since recovered its prestige. Indeed it has become a synonym for the anti-philosopher.

The death of Condorcet in the storm of the Revolution marks the apogee of the *Philosophes*. He was not the last of them. The *Philosophe* is a perennial type. The early H. G. Wells, G. B. Shaw, Bertrand Russell, the Webbs perpetuated the breed beyond France more than a hundred years after Jeremy Bentham and the Mills, father and son. Even in the land of their earliest fame the *Philosophes* were far more numerous and multifarious than might be indicated by the contents table of the present essay. It might be said of them, with especial truth, that *chaque homme porte la forme entière de la condition humaine*. Theirs was a race peculiarly fitted for social intercourse and the traffic of ideas, more especially ideas susceptible of clear expression. 'Whatever is not clear is not French,' it has been said. This may have entailed the sacrifice of a certain amount of depth and subtlety, but it carried with it a compensatory gain in breadth and immediate influence. The French language itself, purged of accretions to an extent far exceeding the philosophic and poetical tongues of the Germans and the English, has an extraordinary dexterity and mobility in the handling of ideas. Like the Greeks, the French think socially and think aloud. As Henry James put it, they are 'intensely audible', generously communicative, ardently persuasive. Such fluency might be supposed to involve corruption by the easy importation of neologisms. Yet, until recent times, the language preserved a purity obsessively, even fanatically. As late as the First World War an obscure French official would refuse to append his name to an order framed by an invader of his country, not because the words were those of an invader but simply because they were bad French. An English reader will commonly avoid disagreeing with an English writer by saying that he does not understand him. In the past such evasion was impossible in French. That rare phenomenon, the incompetent French writer of French, revealed himself in every line, and the fact that it was necessary to search out his meaning told his countrymen straight away that he was talking nonsense.

It is thus that the *Philosophe* is especially accessible to criticism. Rarely does he leave anyone in doubt as to his meaning. 'I think I see what poor Kant would be at,' said James Mill, and we may still wonder whether he did. With Fontenelle or Condillac, with Diderot or Helvétius, we know at once whether we are on the right track, whether the critic has got hold of the right end of the stick. Exposition or criticism of the *Philosophes* is normally downright and resounding. We can make up our minds quickly and easily, and the subject of the discussion can rarely evade pursuit. There are indeed few subjects upon which people have held and do hold, more positive, not to say dogmatic, opinions. The *Philosophes* fully intended to be understood at once by ordinarily intelligent people. It was to such people that they addressed themselves, for their intention was to convert the world. 'Truth is manifest,' they seem to say, and to go on promptly to assume that for truth to triumph little more is needed than the destruction of error. History has shown it to be their principal illusion. But their happy career of onslaught upon error was the main source of their vitality. The cumulative force of their onslaught, breath-taking, even naïve, as it was, greatly helped to clear the world of cant, and the world has greatly benefited by their gay irreverence. Much of the solemnity they dispelled has never recovered its dominance over man's fearful mind.

In all this they were an episode, something swift and transient. The breath was scarcely out of their bodies when fear returned and the world darkened again with the clouds of repentance. It was the French Revolution that signalled the return of a measure of solemnity, the Revolution and the contest of the Dynasts which followed. For a brief moment man had looked around him at the brightening skies and then had crept away to hide his head. He has never quite recovered his nerve. The experience of the Enlightenment, of which the *Philosophes* were the spearhead, was perhaps too exhilarating, too evocative of the *hubris* which seems to afflict every festival of man's reason. Is this to say anything more than that they were too often content with the superficial? Superficial they often were. They would sacrifice much to a jest. Many of their jests, however, have lodged themselves permanently in the memory of Western man, enlivening the flagging mind in duller days, keeping alive the remembrance of happier days before the sun went in again. The years of jesting were to retain a prophylactic value long after the onset of twilight. How dark must the world be to forget *Le Rêve de d'Alembert* or *Le Neveu de Rameau*?

And when the laughing stops, are we to suppose that the works of the *Philosophes* remain to us like a deserted ballroom when the music is silent and the revellers gone? Their successors, the Romantics, certainly invited us to remember them like that, those deep-feeling and often tragic characters of England and Germany whose day dawned with the French Revolution and the great wars of the nations. The works of the *Philosophes*, said Thomas Carlyle in 1833, 'the importance of which is already fast exhausting itself', occupy whole acres of typography, and would occupy the whole of the reading-life of Old Parr, whereas the Acts of the Christian Apostles (as distinct from those of the Parisian Church of Antichrist) may be read in an hour and have been so read for eighteen centuries. 'The shallow Enlightenment' was to become the habitual, almost the unexamined, title of the movement to which they belonged. It required another German, after the onset of unreason in the twentieth century, to initiate their re-examination. Ernst Cassirer published *The Philosophy of the Enlightenment* in German (*Die Philosophie der*

F 2

Aufklärung) at Tübingen in 1932, almost precisely a century after Carlyle's Diderot. Cassirer recalled us to the historic truth:

> Instead of assuming a derogatory air we must take courage and measure our powers against those of the age of the Enlightenment. . . The age which venerated reason and science as man's highest faculty cannot and must not be lost even for us. We must find a way not only to see that age in its own shape but to release again those original forces which brought forth and moulded this shape.

Its motto was, as Kant said, *Sapere aude* – dare to know. It announced man's exodus from his self-imposed tutelage, from his inability without fear and indecision to use his own mind. And for the first time in history an intellectual movement for the emancipation of man was a movement not for the emancipation of a few, the rich, the 'chosen', or the highly educated. What the Apostles of the Christian revelation had once done to change the old pagan world by establishing the gospel of the freedom and equality of the souls of all men, slave and free, this the Apostles of the Parisian Church of Antichrist (sometimes called 'the new pagans') had sought to do for their minds: *'pour changer la façon commune de penser'* they called it. In the larger perspectives of history, however, the 'Anti-Philosophers' may well appear to have been among the principal makers of the modern mind.

CRITICAL BIBLIOGRAPHY

GENERAL

The anti-philosophers, or *Philosophes* of eighteenth-century France, are the French aspect of the movement generally known as the Enlighten-ment (in French *l'Éclaircissement*, or the Enlightenment of Europe in the *Siècle des Lumières*). It was said at the time that Europe was full of ideas and they were all French. This was an exaggeration, but a French writer has considered the thesis in *L'Europe française au siècle des lumières*. Louis Réau's book was published in Paris in 1938 as a volume in the series 'L'Évolution de l'humanité' edited by H. Berr.

Some leading works on the Enlightenment in general are: Ernst Cassirer, *The Philosophy of the Enlightenment* (Princeton, 1951; original German edition, Tübingen, 1932); Lester G. Crocker, *The Age of Crisis: Man and World in Eighteenth-Century French Thought* (Baltimore, 1959) and *Nature and Culture, Ethical Thought in the French Enlightenment* (Baltimore, 1963); Peter Gay, *The Enlightenment, The Rise of Modern Paganism* (New York, 1967), pages 423–552 of which contain a valuable bibliographical essay; the late Paul Hazard's two volumes are indispen-sable: *La Crise de la conscience européenne* (Paris, 1935), which is obtainable in Penguin Books, translated by J. Lewis May, as *The European Mind, 1680–1715*, and *La Pensée européenne au XVIIIᵉ siècle* (1946) translated by the same hand, also in Penguins (*European Thought in the Eighteenth Century* 1954); older works, but still useful are Lord Morley's *Diderot and the Encyclopedists* (2 vols., 1878), Hippolyte Taine's *Les Origines de la France contemporaine: l'ancien régime* (Paris, 1891), J. B. Bury's *The Idea of Progress* (1932), and Kingsley Martin's *French Liberal Thought in the Eighteenth Century* (new ed., 1962). Carl Becker's *The Heavenly City of the Eighteenth-Century Philosophers* (Yale, 1932) carries a certain line of argument further than can be justified. J. P. Belin's *Le Mouvement philosophique de 1748–1789* (Paris, 1913) remains useful. In the present century we have Charles Frankel's *The Faith of Reason* (New York,

1948), R. V. Sampson's *Progress in the Age of Reason* (1956), and the late Alfred Cobban's *In Search of Humanity* (1960). One of the most recent and most valuable studies is Peter Gay's *The Party of Humanity* (1964). Betty Behrens has written a delightful short study of the background of the movement in her recent book, *The Ancien Régime*. J. S. Spink, *French Free Thought from Gassendi to Voltaire* (1960), is also immensely useful.

Valuable studies of some special aspects are: R. R. Palmer, *Catholics and Unbelievers in Eighteenth-Century France* (Princeton, 1959), the late Canon Charles Raven's Gifford Lectures of 1951 on *Natural Religion and Christian Theology* (Cambridge, 1953) and Maxime Leroy's *Histoire des idées sociales en France*, I, *de Montesquieu à Robespierre*, 'Bibliothèque des Idées' (Paris, 1947). For the scientific and technological background, reference should be made to A. Wolf's *History of Science, Technology and Philosophy in the Eighteenth Century* (1960). For the social and historical connections of science, *The Origins of Modern Science* by Sir Herbert Butterfield (especially chapters IX and X) is of particular value to historians. Two other studies dealing with a favourite theme of great prominence in the period of the French Enlightenment are: A. O. Lovejoy's *The Great Chain of Being* (Harvard, 1936) and *Primitivism and Progress in the Eighteenth Century* by L. Whitney (Baltimore, 1934).

1 THE GRAND CHAIN

For the apposition of *Philosophes* and philosophers, there is fruitful matter for reflection in Michael Oakeshott's work, *Experience and its Modes* (1933), especially the opening chapter, and 'The New Bentham' (*Scrutiny*, 1 no. 2). On the character of the *Philosophe* according to Diderot, see his article on ENCYCLOPÉDIE, reprinted in John Lough's volume, *The Encyclopedia of Diderot and d'Alembert* (Cambridge, 1954), and his *Pensées sur l'interprétation de la nature*, Pensées XVI, XIX, XXIII and XL (reprinted in John Lough's edition of Diderot, *Selected Philosophical Writings* (Cambridge, 1953). See also '*Le Philosophe*, texts and interpretation', by H. Dieckmann in *Washington University Studies*, new series: 'Language and Literature', no. 18 (St Louis, 1948).

The slant, and the monopolising interests of the *Philosophes* may best be judged by reading d'Alembert's *Discours préliminaire* to the Encyclopedia, of which there is a handy translation in the paperback series, 'The Library of Liberal Arts' (New York, 1963). The French text is edited by F. Picavet (Paris, 1894).

2. FONTENELLE

There is a brief life of Fontenelle, containing some of the most notorious anecdotes about him, at the beginning of Paul Janet's little volume, Fontenelle, *Choix d'éloges*, in the series 'Classiques français' (Paris, 1880).

The best French text of his *Entretiens sur la pluralité des mondes* is that edited by Robert Shackleton (Oxford, 1955). This volume also contains his *Digression sur les anciens et les modernes*. The edition edited by Thierry Maulnier has an excellent introductory essay to which I have been much indebted. The Nonesuch Press published a most attractive edition of J. Glanvill's translation, with a prologue by David Garnett, in 1929, entitled *A Plurality of Worlds*.

Fontenelle's *De l'origine des fables* is edited by J.-R. Carré (Paris, 1932), and his *Histoires des oracles* by L. Maigron (Paris, 1934). The latter has also been edited more recently by M. Bouchard (Paris, 1947). The standard study of Fontenelle is *La Philosophie de Fontenelle, ou le sourire de la raison*, by J.-R. Carré (Paris, 1932). The typical French work, slightly older, is L. Maigron's *Fontenelle, l'homme, l'œuvre, l'influence* (Paris, 1906). There is also *Fontenelle* by A. Laborde-Milaà (Paris, 1905).

The whole question of *Les Mondes imaginaires et les mondes réels* was exhaustively dealt with by C. Flammarion in his book of that title (Paris, 1865), and the quarrel between Ancients and Moderns by A. H. Rigault in his *Histoire de la querelle des anciens et des modernes* (Paris, 1856). A modern discussion by G. McColley is to be found in *The Annals of Science* (1936), entitled 'The Seventeenth-Century Doctrine of a Plurality of Worlds'.

An important discussion of Fontenelle's place in the evolution of modern thought may be found in Sir Herbert Butterfield's work, *The Origins of Modern Science* (chap. IX). J. B. Bury has a useful chapter on him in *The Idea of Progress* (chap. V), both of which have been cited in the 'general' section above.

Fontenelle should be seen against the tradition of *libertin* literature in France, and for this purpose recourse may be had to R. Pintard's *Le Libertinage érudit dans la première moitié du XVIIᵉ siècle* (2 vols, Paris,

1943). The great figure in this tradition is of course Cyrano de Bergerac, whose *œuvres libertines* have been edited by F. Lachèvre (2 vols, Paris, 1921). Reference of a more general kind may be made to Gustave Lanson's 'Origines et premières manifestations de l'esprit philosophique dans la littérature française de 1765 à 1748, in *Revue des cours et conférences* (1907–9).

H. L. Edsall in *Fontenelle and Voltaire*, 'Yale Studies' (New Haven, 1946), studies the succession as distinct from the ancestry.

3. PARIS, 1715

Although Louis-Sébastien Mercier's book, *Le Nouveau Paris* (1797), is concerned with the life of the city mainly towards the end of the century, the early part portrays the city in the middle of the period. An English translation by W. and E. Jackson, under the title *The Picture of Paris*, may be found in the Broadway Library (1929). Helen Simpson's abridged version is entitled *The Waiting City* (1933).

Other works relevant to this chapter are G. Mongrédien's *La Vie de société au XVIIIᵉ siècle* (Paris, 1950), and F. C. Green's *Eighteenth-Century France: Six Essays* (1929). J. F. Marmontel's *Mémoires* (4 vols., Paris, 1805) are full of references to the life of that society; there is a single-volume version in the Broadway Library (1930).

4. VOLTAIRE AND NEWTON

Voltaire's advocacy of 'the English philosophy' is most readily seen in his *Lettres philosophiques*, of which the most convenient edition is that edited by Raymond Naves, in 'Classiques Garnier' (Paris, 1951). The general question of Newton in France is well discussed by Pierre Brunet in his *Introduction des théories de Newton en France* (Paris, 1931). The extensive study of Voltaire's position in society in his century is to be found in G. le Desnoiresterre's *Voltaire et la société au XVIIIᵉ siècle* (2nd ed., 8 vols., Paris, 1871–6). Voltaire's relations with the Encyclopedists is the subject of a useful study by Raymond Naves, *Voltaire et l'Encyclopédie* (Paris, 1938). His letters have been edited in well over a hundred volumes by Theodore Besterman, who also produced a *Selection* (Geneva, 1952). Of the lives, A. Bellessort's *Essai sur Voltaire* (14th ed.,

1933) is in many ways preferable: others in fairly short form by Lord Morley (1871), H. N. Brailsford (Oxford, 1935), J. M. Robertson (1922) are useful but not outstanding. His politics have been made the subject of a brilliant study by Peter Gay, *Voltaire's Politics* (Princeton and Oxford, 1959). There is a useful study of his position as a writer of history by J. H. Brumfitt, *Voltaire, Historian* (Oxford, 1958). For the student of the *Philosophes*, his *conte*, *Micromégas*, is particularly impor‹ tant. This and a good selection of the other *contes* were published by the Cambridge University Press in 1951, and edited by F. C. Green, under the title *Voltaire: Choix de contes*. There is also a separate edition of *Micromégas*, edited by Ira O. Wade (Princeton, 1950). Voltaire's per‹ sonal Encyclopedia, *Dictionnaire philosophique*, 1764, may be found in the 'Classiques Garnier'.

The repository of a large number of Voltairean studies is the long succession of volumes edited by Theodore Besterman called *Studies on Voltaire and the Eighteenth Century*. Though a great deal of the work in these volumes relates fairly directly to Voltaire and his works, they also contain a lot of work on other figures and topics of his age. Anyone working on the intellectual life of the century should make regular use of them. Some thirty volumes are already in being.

For other figures central to this chapter, Bayle's Dictionary has been made to yield a fairly representative selection in a volume of that title edited by E. A. Beller and M. Lee (Princeton, 1952). Howard Robinson's *Bayle the Sceptic* (Columbia, 1931) is good secondary material. More specialised is *Pierre Bayle, le philosophe de Rotterdam, études et documents*, edited by Paul Dibon (Amsterdam, 1959). For Montesquieu, *De l'esprit des lois* is in 'Classiques Garnier' (Paris, 1949). Perhaps his alliance with the *Philosophes* is more apparent in his *Lettres persanes*, available in many editions.

5. CONDILLAC AND LOCKE

There are many editions of Locke's *Essay Concerning the Human Under‹ standing*. A paperback edition is available in Collins's Fontana Library. Books I and II are most relevant here.

The works of Condillac are available in three volumes, *Œuvres philo‹ sophiques*, ed. George Le Roy (Paris, 1947–51). For the general reader, Roger Lefèvre's *Condillac, ou la joie de vie*, contains selections with explication. This little volume is in Seghers's series, 'Philosophie de tous les temps' (Paris, 1966). Useful for our present purpose is Geraldine Carr's translation, *Treatise on the Sensations* (1930), as is Georges Lyons's *Extrait raisonné du Traité des sensations* (Paris, 1921). Raymond Lenoir's *Condillac* (Paris, 1924) is a sober study but hardly inspiring for the general reader. As an example of the eighteenth-century cult of the animated statue, there is André-François Boureau-Deslandes's *Pigmalion, ou la statue animée* (London, 1741). Isabel F. Knight's *The Geometric Spirit* (Yale University Press, 1968) bears the sub-title *Condillac and the French Enlightenment*.

6. THE MAN OF LANGRES

Indispensable are the texts: *Œuvres philosophiques*, ed. Paul Vernière 'Classiques Garnier' (Paris, 1956), and Diderot, *Selected philosophical writings* (in French), ed. John Lough (Cambridge, 1953). There is an English translation by M. Jourdain of some of the latter, *Early Philosophical Works* (1916). More readily accessible is L. W. Tancock's translation of *Le Neveu de Rameau* and *Le Rêve de d'Alembert* in the Penguin Classics (L 173, 1966).

The best English life of Diderot is that by A. M. Wilson: *Diderot: The Testing Years: 1713–1759* (New York, 1957). For Diderot's early life there are Franco Venturi's *Jeunesse de Diderot* (Paris, 1939) and J. Pommier's *Diderot avant Vincennes* (Paris, 1939).

Of older works, Lord Morley's *Diderot* (1878) and Carlyle's essay, 'Diderot' (1833), included in his *Critical and Miscellaneous Essays*, were pioneer studies in English. Other lives are A. Billy's *Diderot* (Paris, 1932), I. K. Luppol's *Diderot, ses idées philosophiques* (Paris, 1936), D. Mornet's *Diderot, l'homme et l'œuvre* (Paris, 1941), H. Lefebvre's *Diderot, hier et aujourd'hui* (Paris, 1949), and G. Lester Crocker's *The Embattled Philosopher* (London, 1955). Among many valuable studies are J. Thomas's *L'Humanisme de Diderot* (Paris, 1938), *Diderot Studies* edited by O. E. Fellows and N. L. Torrey (Syracuse, 1949); and (of special importance) Aram Vartanian's excellent study, *Descartes and Diderot* (Princeton, 1953).

For Diderot's debt to Shaftesbury, the essay contributed by Dorothy B. Schlegel to vol. XXVII of Theodore Besterman's *Studies on Voltaire and the eighteenth century* (Geneva, 1963) will repay study. Basil Willey has some useful introductory remarks on Shaftesbury in his *The Eighteenth-Century Background* (1946), chap. IV.

7. VINCENNES

The texts referred to in this chapter are *Lettre sur les aveugles,* and *Pensées sur l'interprétation de la nature.* The *Lettre* is best read in Paul Vernière's collection, *Œuvres philosophiques.* It can be read in English in Jourdain's *Early Philosophical Works.* The *Pensées* may also be read in Vernière's volume, but the most convenient edition is probably John Lough's *Selected Philosophical Writings.* All these have been cited for the previous chapter.

For Malesherbes, see the life by P. Grosclaude, *Malesherbes* (Paris, 1961), or J. M. S. Allison's *Malesherbes* (New Haven, 1938).

For Diderot as 'the *Socrate imaginaire*' see Jean Seznec's *Essais sur Diderot et l'antiquité,* chap. 1 (Oxford, 1957).

For Diderot and Rousseau at Vincennes, see Rousseau's *Confessions,* bk. VIII, of which there are many editions.

For Buffon, if the reader does not wish to read some of his *Histoire naturelle* in the original 127 volumes, or in the *Œuvres complètes* (Paris, 1854–5), Paul Bonnefon's essay prefacing his *Pages choisies de Buffon* (Paris, 1922) is an excellent introduction for the general reader. There is also a pleasantly old-fashioned volume in Émile Faguet's 'Collection des Classiques Populaires' edited by Henri Lebasteur and garnished with some surprising illustrations of birds and beasts. The supercession of mathematics by natural science in the eighteenth century is brilliantly dealt with by Ernst Cassirer in his *Philosophy of the Enlightenment,* chap. II, cited at the beginning of this bibliography.

8. LE RÊVE DE D'ALEMBERT

The text of Diderot on d'Alembert, including *Le Rêve,* is easily obtainable in John Lough's volume of Diderot's *Selected Philosophical Writings* (1953). These works, together with *Le Neveu de Rameau,* are obtainable in a convenient translation in Penguin Classics. These books have been cited in the section on Chapter 6.

For Julie de Lespinasse the best source is her letters, *Lettres de Julie de Lespinasse,* ed. E. Asse (Paris, 1882). An English translation by Katherine Prescott Wormeley was published in 1903. There are studies by C. Jebb,

A Star of the Salons, Julie de Lespinasse (1908), S. G. Tallentyne, *The Women of the Salons* (New York and London, 1926), and P. de Ségur, *Julie de Lespinasse* (Paris, 1906). Sainte-Beuve's essay in *Causeries du lundi*, vol. II, is well known, and there are many editions.

9. MAN A MACHINE

The best text of *L'Homme machine* is the critical edition by Aram Vartanian (Princeton, 1960). La Mettrie's *Œuvres philosophiques* were first published in three volumes in Amsterdam in 1774. H. R. R. Paquet's *Essai sur La Mettrie* was published in Paris in 1873. There is also E. Du Bois-Reymond, *La Mettrie* (Berlin, 1875). Vartanian has a valuable article in *The Journal of the History of Ideas*, XI no. 3 (June 1950) pp. 259–286, on 'Trembley's Polyp, La Mettrie, and eighteenth-century French materialism'. The progress from the beast-machine to the man-machine is discussed in *From Beast-machine to Man-machine*, by Leonora C. Rosenfeld (New York, 1941). The Cartesian mechanism is interestingly discussed in an article by S. V. Keeling in *Philosophy*, IX (January, 1934) pp. 51–66. Perhaps the best-known recent work, however, is by Gilbert Ryle in his discussion of what he has called 'The Ghost in the Machine' in his *The Concept of Mind* (1949), pp. 18–22. The birth of mechanism is traced by Robert Lenoble in *Mersenne, ou la naissance du mécanisme* (Paris, 1943). The whole question of the beast-mechanism is discussed most profoundly in Sir Charles Sherrington's masterpiece, *Man on his Nature* (Cambridge, 1940).

10. THE CRITICAL DECADE

Charles-Pinot Duclos: *Considérations sur les mœurs de ce siècle*, was published precisely at the mid-century mark. The most useful edition for the student is that edited by F. C. Green, and published by the Cambridge University Press in 1946. The presentation of Palissot's satire, *Les Philosophes*, may be studied after reference to the bibliography of Chapters 1, 2 and 3 above and the notes to this chapter below. For the animosities of the learned societies and academies see Jean Seznec's

Essais sur Diderot et l'antiquité (cited above) especially Essai v. Gibbon's *Essai sur l'étude de la littérature* belongs to 1761, and is to be found in his *Miscellaneous Works* (1796), vol. II. A. Momignano's discussion of Gibbon is to be found in 'Gibbon's Contribution to Historical Method' in *Historia*, vol. II, part 4 (1954) pp. 450–63. Seznec's notes to his fifth lecture are the best reference for the intellectual history of the decade.

D'Alembert's reflections on the significance of the mid-century mark are to be found in his *Éléments de philosophie* (see *Mélanges de littérature, d'histoire, et de philosophie*, 1759, vol. IV pp. 3–6). The celebrated passage cited was used by Ernst Cassirer in opening his *Philosophy of the Enlightenment*, where it is quoted at length on pp. 3–4.

11, 12, 13, 14, 15. (PART III: THE ENCYCLOPEDIA)

For the Encyclopedia, Jacques Proust's *Diderot et L'Encyclopédie* (Armand Colin, 1967) is the latest and finest work. The reader should try to get access to the original work in seventeen volumes, and sample some of the articles. Perusal of the additional volumes of plates is also to be recommended. These large but fascinating volumes are to be found in most learned libraries which existed in the eighteenth century. An alternative course is to secure a copy of John Lough's slender volume, *The Encyclopédie of Diderot and d'Alembert: Selected Articles* (Cambridge, 1954), and to have recourse to the original volumes when disappointed.

Works about the Encyclopedia since the second centenary of publication in 1751 are headed by *Un Audacieux Message: L'Encyclopédie* by P. Grosclaude (Paris, 1951). The bicentenary evoked many publications: 'Diderot et l'Encyclopédie', in the *Revue d'histoire littéraire de la France* (July–September 1951); 'L'Encyclopédie et son rayonnement à l'étranger', in *Cahiers de l'Association Internationale des Études Françaises* (May 1952); and a series of articles in the *Revue d'histoire des sciences et de leurs applications* (July–December 1951) which were later republished in book form as *L'Encyclopédie et le progrès des sciences et des techniques* (1952). The lectures delivered at the Sorbonne in March and April 1952 were published in a special number of *Annales de l'Université de Paris* (October 1952).

Older works of much value are: Joseph Legras, *Diderot et l'Encyclopédie* (Amiens, 1928), René Hubert's *Les Sciences sociales et l'Encyclopédie* (Paris, 1923). A more recent work, *The Censoring of Diderot's Encyclopédie and the Re-established Text* by D. H. Gordon and N. L. Torrey

(New York, 1947) tells a dramatic story. Voltaire's version of the con‑
fiscation is to be found in his volume of short pieces, *Le Taureau blanc*,
ed. R. Pomeau (Paris, 1956). This delightful work was first translated by
Jeremy Bentham in 1774. A translation is included in D. I. Woolf's
edition of *Zadig and Other Romances* (1928), and in *The White Bull* by
C. E. Vulliamy (1929).

Palissot's satire on the *Philosophes* may be read about in *La Vie et
l'œuvres de Palissot* by Daniel Delafarge (Paris, 1912), especially chaps.
3 to 6. The original comedy may be found in *Le Répertoire du théâtre
français*, 3ᵉ ordre, vol. VI (Paris, 1819).

Voltaire et l'Encyclopédie, by Raymond Naves, cited above, and his
Rousseau et l'Encyclopédie (Paris, 1928) reveal a good deal of the in‑fighting
of the day. The critical part played by Malesherbes in the story makes it
necessary to read some study of that key‑figure. Two are cited in the
bibliography to Chapter 7 above.

For d'Alembert, see R. Grimsley's *Jean d'Alembert* (Oxford, 1963).
Inseparable from d'Alembert is Julie de Lespinasse, and for her life see
the biographies and editions of her letters listed for Chapter 8 above.

There is a useful, though mainly quantitative, study of the Encyclo‑
pedists' treatment of the Christian religion in J. E. Barker's study of that
title (1941).

16. THE POLITICS OF THE PHILOSOPHES

One may form some conclusions on this subject by examining the
articles on legal and political topics in John Lough's selection of articles
from the Encyclopedia, cited above. Other documentary material is to
be found in Diderot's *Réfutation suivie de l'ouvrage d'Helvétius intitulé
L'Homme*, which may be found in his *Œuvres philosophiques*, edited
Paul Vernière, cited for Chapter 6. Other works to consult are Morley's
Diderot and Peter Gay's *Politics of Voltaire*. The chief contribution of the
Philosophes to politics was their great political act, the production of the
Encyclopedia. Kingsley Martin's *French Liberal Thought in the Eighteenth
Century* has a pronounced political slant throughout. There is an article
on 'The Development and Scope of Diderot's Political Thought' by
Arthur M. Wilson in vol. 27 of Besterman's *Studies on Voltaire in the
eighteenth century*.

17. HELVÉTIUS

The works of Helvétius were published collectively in Paris in 1818. Vol. 1 contains *De l'esprit*. *Helvétius, sa vie et son œuvre*, by A. Keim (Paris, 1907) is ponderous but informative. Of modern works, the best is by D. W. Smith's *Helvétius* (Oxford, 1965). It bears the sub-title: 'A study in persecution'. Today, Helvétius matters mostly in the history of education, and it is to that aspect that Ian Cumming's book, *Helvétius* (1955), is devoted. Lord Morley's chapter in the second volume of his *Diderot* (chap. XIII) is a useful exposition.

For this, too, see James Mill's *Essay on Education*, which is reprinted in F. A. Cavanagh's volume *James and John Mill on Education* (Cambridge, 1931).

The Marxist use of Helvétius is illustrated by the second of G. V. Plekhanov's *Essays in the History of Materialism* (1896).

18. LE MAÎTRE D'HÔTEL DE LA PHILOSOPHIE

D'Holbach is discussed in chapter 14 of the second volume of Morley's *Diderot*. He is also the subject of the first of G. V. Plekhanov's *Essays in the History of Materialism*. The most useful work, however, is René Hubert's *Baron d'Holbach et ses amis, choix de textes* (Paris, 1928). For comment and historical 'placing' there is an excellent account in W. H. Wickwar's *Baron d'Holbach, a prelude to the French Revolution* (1935). More recent is Pierre Naville's *D'Holbach et la scientifique au XVIIIe siècle* (Paris, 1943).

General reference should be made to Friedrich Albert Lange's *History of Materialism*, tr. E. C. Thomas (3 vols., London 1879–81).

19. ROUSSEAU

For his early association with Diderot and the future *Philosophes*, see Rousseau's *Confessions*, particularly Books VII and VIII (L. 33 in the Penguin Classics).

The cardinal document, however, is Rousseau's prize-winning essay of

1750, *Si le rétablissement des sciences et des arts a contribué à épurer les mœurs*. A useful English version is that included in G. D. H. Cole's edition of *The Social Contract* ⟨No. 660 in Everyman's Library⟩. Scarcely less important for his relations with the *Philosophes* is his letter to d'Alembert on his article, GENÈVE, in the Encyclopedia, 1758. See *Rousseau et l'Encyclopédie*, by René Hubert ⟨Paris, 1928⟩ and R. Grimsley's *Jean d'Alembert* ⟨Oxford, 1963⟩. Ernst Cassirer's study of *The Question of Jean-Jacques Rousseau*, translated with an introduction by Peter Gay ⟨New York, 1954⟩ is of great importance.

20. THE MARQUIS'S OMELETTE

The document here is Condorcet's *Sketch for a Historical Picture of the Progress of the Human Mind* which, translated by June Barraclough and with an introduction by Stuart Hampshire, was published in Weidenfeld & Nicolson's 'Library of Ideas' in 1955. There is an older edition of the *Esquisse* in French edited by O. H. Prior ⟨Paris, 1933⟩. A. Condorcet O'Connor and M. F. Arago edited the *Œuvres complètes* ⟨12 vols., Paris, 1847⟩.

Studies of Condorcet are: F. Alengry, *Condorcet* ⟨Paris, 1904⟩; F. Buisson, *Condorcet* ⟨Paris, 1932⟩; J. Bouissonouse, *Condorcet* ⟨Paris, 1962⟩; Sir James Frazer, *Condorcet on the Progress of the Human Mind* ⟨Oxford, 1933⟩; J. S. Schapiro, *Condorcet and the Rise of Liberalism* ⟨New York, 1934⟩.

There are useful articles and essays by: Alexander Koyre: 'Condorcet', in the *Journal of the History of Ideas*, IX, no. 2 ⟨April, 1948⟩; John Morley, 'Condorcet' in *Critical Miscellanies*, II ⟨1886⟩; C. A. Sainte-Beuve, 'Condorcet' in *Causeries du lundi*, vol. III; Henri Sée, 'Condorcet, ses idées et son rôle politique' in *Le Revue de synthèse historique*, X, 1905.

Condorcet is discussed in: Carl Becker's *Heavenly City of the Eighteenth-Century Philosophers*, J. B. Bury's *Idea of Progress*, Charles Frankel's *The Faith of Reason*, and Kingsley Martin's *French Liberal Thought in the Eighteenth Century*. For the above see the first section of this bibliography. Daniel Mornet also dealt with him in *Les Origines intellectuelles de la révolution française* ⟨3rd ed., Paris, 1934⟩.

Other works referred to in the present chapter are: Giles-Gaston Granger, *La Mathématique sociale du Marquis de Condorcet* ⟨Paris, 1956⟩; Duncan Black's *The Theory of Committees and Elections* ⟨Cambridge,

1958); A. R. J. Turgot's *Discours sur les progrès successifs de l'esprit humain* (1750). The latter is, of course, to be found in *Œuvres* (9 vols., Paris, 1808–11). There is a valuable study by Douglas Dakin (*Turgot and the Ancien Régime in France* (1939), and a selection from his writings in *Textes choisis* edited by P. Vigreux (Paris, 1947).

Epilogue

Louis Réau's *L'Europe française*, cited at the beginning of this bibliography, provides material for forming an impression of the 'style' of eighteenth-century France. For the language, reference should be made to C. F. de Vaugelas, *Remarques sur la langue française*, ed. J. Streicher (Paris, 1934). The 'life-quality' of an age is best discovered by reading its literature, looking at its pictures and sculpture, of all of which it is the residuum. There is some splendid assistance in all this to be gained from *The Age of Rococo* by A. Schönberger and H. Soehner (1960).

INDEX